Why can't computer books be easier to understand?

Not all of us want to become computer professionals, but we do want to have fun with our computers and be productive. The new *Simple Guides* cover the popular topics in computing. More importantly, they are simple to understand. Each book in the series introduces the main features of a topic and shows you how to get the most from your PC.

Simple Guides – No gimmicks, no jargon, no fuss

Available in the *Simple Guides* series:

The Internet	Building a website
Searching the Internet	Creating and using spreadsheets
The PC	Putting audio and video on your website
Office 2000	Writing for your website
Windows 98	Dreamweaver 4
E-commerce	Flash 5 for Windows
Digital cameras, scanning and using images	Visual Basic

A simple guide to
HTML

**Brian Salter and
Naomi Langford-Wood**

An imprint of PEARSON EDUCATION

Pearson Education Limited

Head Office:
Edinburgh Gate
Harlow
Essex CM20 2JE
Tel: +44 (0)1279 623623
Fax: +44 (0)1279 431059

London Office:
128 Long Acre
London WC2E 9AN
Tel: +44 (0)20 7447 2000
Fax: +44 (0)20 7240 5771
website: www.it-minds.com

Published in Great Britain in 2002
© Pearson Education Limited 2002

ISBN 0-130-08843-9

The rights of Brian Salter and Naomi Langford-Wood to be identified as the authors of this work have been asserted by them in accordance with the Copyright, Designs and Patents Act 1988.

British Library Cataloguing-in-Publication Data
A catalogue record for this book can be obtained from the British Library.

All rights reserved. No part of this publication may be reproduced, stored in a retrieval system, or transmitted, in any form, or by any means, electronic, mechanical, photocopying, recording or otherwise, without prior written permission from the publisher.

Many of the designations used by manufacturers and sellers to distinguish their products are claimed as trademarks. Pearson Education Limited has made every attempt to supply trademark information about manufacturers and their products mentioned in this book. All Web sites reproduced herein are copyright of their owners.

10 9 8 7 6 5 4 3 2 1

Typeset by Pantek Arts Ltd, Maidstone, Kent.
Printed and bound in Great Britain.

The publishers' policy is to use paper manufactured from sustainable forests.

Contents

Introduction xii
What is in this book xii
Conventions and icons xiii
About the authors xiv

1 Document structure 1

What is HTML? 2
Why bother with the code at all? 7
A basic page 9
`<HTML>` 12
`<HEAD>` 13
`<BODY>` 13
The other stuff 13
`<TITLE>` 15
A word of warning 15

2 Text formatting ... 19

Headings ... 20
Paragraphs ... 22
Physical styles ... 25
Logical styles ... 26
Preformatted text ... 28
Special characters ... 28
Text alignment ... 30
Fonts ... 31

3 Graphics, colour and background ... 35

`<IMG>` tag ... 38
Aligning text with images ... 42
Controlling text wrapping ... 43
Image spacing ... 46
Image scaling ... 48
Image previews ... 48
Image alternatives ... 49
Background images ... 50
Background colours ... 51
Horizontal rules ... 51

4 Multimedia ... 57

Sound ... 58
Video ... 63
Flash and Shockwave ... 63
Java applets ... 64

5 Links and image maps ... 67

HREF ... 68
Relative path names ... 69
Absolute path names ... 70
Linking to Web pages ... 71
Linking to specific locations ... 72
Special characters ... 73
Mailto: ... 74
Using images as links ... 75
Image maps ... 76

6 Lists ... 81

Numbered lists ... 82
Bulleted lists ... 87

Glossary lists 91
Nesting lists 92

7 Tables 95

Table basics 96
Heading cells 101
Sizing and padding tables 103
Borders 105
Text layout in tables 105
Setting colours and backgrounds 106
Alignment 109
Spanning multiple rows and columns 109
Headers and footers 113
Frame and rule attributes 116

8 Style sheets 119

How style sheets work 120
External style sheets 122
Creating a style sheet 123
Embedded style sheets 125
Cascading? 127

Margins and padding 127
Backgrounds 129
Borders 131
Text appearance 132
Text alignment 133
Inline styles 134

9 Frames 137

What are frames? 138
Target 140
`<BASE>` 144
Framesets 144
`<FRAME>` 146
`<NOFRAMES>` 147
Frame borders 148x

10 Forms 151

Why forms? 152
What's in a form? 152
Buttons 153

Text input 154
Radio buttons 157
Check boxes 158
Resetting values 159
Selections 160
Form methods 162
CGI script 162

11 JavaScript and DHTML 165

JavaScript structure 166
Sourcing JavaScript programs 167
Dynamic HTML 169
Dynamic styles 170
Dynamic content 175
Positioning and animation 177

12 Meta tags 181

What are meta tags? 182
General tags 184
Format 185

DC tags 187
Other tags 188

Appendix: HTML colour equivalents 191

Index 197

Introduction

Ever since the commercial Internet made its appearance just over a decade ago, the world has changed dramatically. Can there really be anyone in the western world who hasn't been touched in some way or another by the World Wide Web? Yet the initial concept of the Web relies on one very simple premise: the ability to navigate from one piece of information to another, jumping through virtual hyperspace.

The core of the Internet is HTML – or HyperText Markup Language. It is the code you can find behind every single web page. And it's all based on a simple set of rules that make the page readable by a browser, whether on PC, Apple Mac, handheld computer, mainframe, UNIX box, or (with a little bit of tweaking) mobile phone device.

Coding an HTML page is relatively easy, so long as you follow the rules; and this book will give you the wherewithal to be able to do just that!

What is in this book

A Simple Guide to HTML helps you to master the basics of HTML so that you can design, create and maintain professional-looking Websites.

Starting with the structure of a simple Web page, we will be looking at:

- Hyperlinks
- Text tags

- Graphics and image maps
- Style sheets
- Tables
- Frames
- Forms
- Metatags
- Javascript

and a whole lot more along the way. You'll find copious screen shots and snippets of code to help you grasp the concepts quickly and easily.

Conventions and icons

Throughout the book we have included notes, each of which is associated with an icon:

These notes provide additional information about the subject concerned.

These notes indicate a variety of shortcuts: keyboard shortcuts, 'Wizard' options, techniques reserved for experts, etc.

These notes warn you of the risks associated with a particular action and, where necessary, show you how to avoid any pitfalls.

About the authors

Brian Salter and Naomi Langford-Wood are 21st-century business experts and practical visionaries. Having come from very different backgrounds, they are specialists in all aspects of communication, motivation, strategy and other business issues including the use of Internet technologies and e-business and the building of powerful online communities; and they are leading international speakers in this arena.

Because of these core skills, they have increasingly found their company (Topspin Group – www.topspin-group.com) in demand for advice on the use of emerging technologies within business, and – in the process – recognised that the cornerstone requirement for all of this commenced with conducting client Internet and communications audits, as a prerequisite to creating effective market positioning and customer-focused business strategies for these clients. This approach has led to commissions by companies worldwide – both 'blue chip' and SMEs – for high-level consultancies and entrepreneurial flair.

Together, Brian and Naomi help companies realise their full potential by incorporating the new technologies into their business processes as painlessly and profitably as possible whilst looking after each company's core assets – its people. Founders of The Association of E-Business Professionals (www.e-biz-pro.org), they are also fellows of the Royal Society of Arts and the Institute of Directors.

Document structure

1

What is HTML?

Why bother with the code at all?

A basic page

`<HTML>`

`<HEAD>`

`<BODY>`

The other stuff

`<TITLE>`

A word of warning

What is HTML?

HTML is a great idea. And like most great ideas its simplicity is staggering. Yet without it we would never have been able to enjoy the benefits of the World Wide Web that we all do these days.

The concept of HTML is that it describes the structure of a document. Most documents have a title, paragraphs, lists, and maybe graphics, videos and sound. You don't need to have a title, just as you don't need graphics or lists, but the document still functions despite such omissions.

In a way, it's rather like working with a word processor. If you're familiar with MS Word, for example, then you will also know about setting styles for paragraphs or headings, creating bulleted lists or numbered lists, changing font colours or font sizes and a whole lot more besides.

HTML does the same for Web pages. It too defines styles for paragraphs and headings, lists and tables. But what it doesn't do is say anything about how a page looks when it is viewed in a browser. All it says is that this line is a heading, or this collection of words behaves like a paragraph, or whatever. The fact that you can view the Web page in any one of a number of browsers is one of the beauties of HTML being cross-platform compatible.

The most common browsers are Microsoft Explorer, Netscape Navigator and Opera (Figure 1.1) but there are quite a few others, some of them peculiar to certain platforms only.

1: Document structure

Figure 1.1 Explorer, Netscape and Opera are the most commonly found browsers.

At the time of writing, both Netscape and Explorer are into their sixth editions, whilst Opera has release 5 out. Not surprisingly, each upgrade to the browser brings in new features, some of which are pertinent to the way HTML defines the page and others not.

We said a moment ago that HTML does not define how a page looks when it is displayed in a browser; and this may be a surprise to many who assume it is the HTML tags that define all the characteristics of a Web page. But in fact HTML defines whether something is, for example, a heading or a paragraph, not how one particular heading is displayed in a browser. That part is down to the browser itself. (We'll see how to get round some of these limitations later in the book.)

For example, let's look at the following three figures, which show one Web page displayed by three different browsers. The first one (Figure 1.2) shows how MS Explorer displays the page. See how the font is sans-serif (in this case Arial Black). Yet in the second screen shot (Figure 1.3) Netscape displays a serif font similar to Times New Roman. You'll probably be unable to see that the colours of the table borders differ markedly from one another. (If we had been viewing either of these on an Apple Mac instead of a PC the overall colours would also have looked different.)

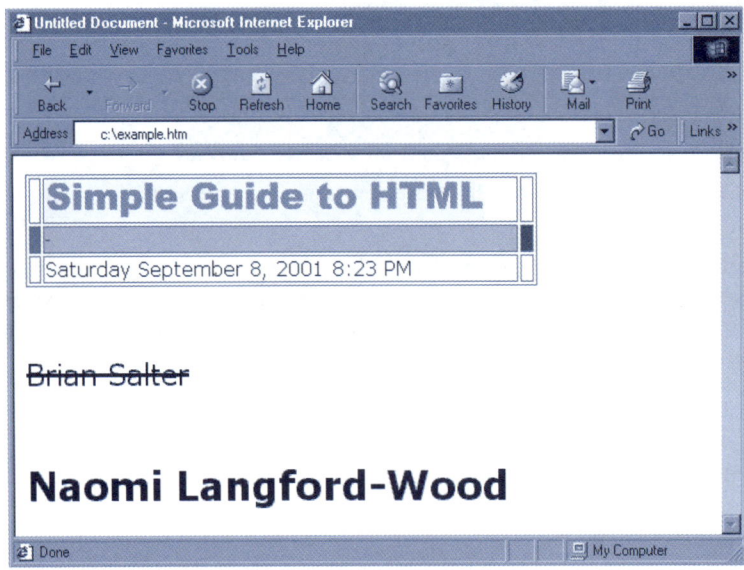

Figure 1.2 A Web page as viewed by MS Explorer.

1: Document structure

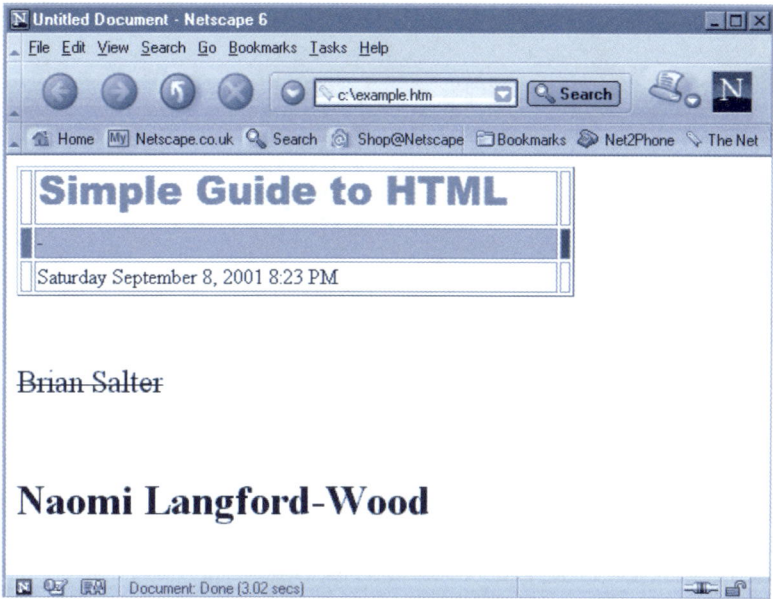

Figure 1.3 The same page viewed in Netscape version 6.

Worse is to come, though. Surely no-one is still using the very first version of Netscape Navigator, which was still in common use just five years ago? But if they are, then our Web page will look like Figure 1.4.

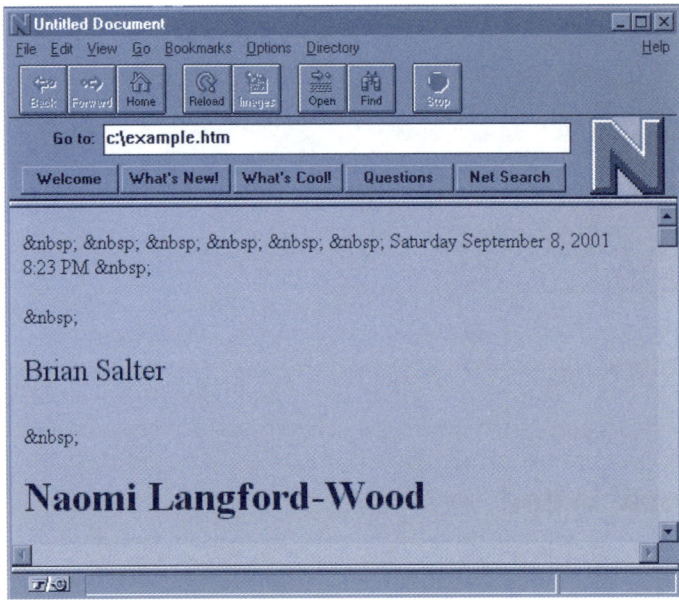

Figure 1.4 Netscape Navigator version 1 simply cannot cope with a very simple page layout.

The problem here is that this particular version doesn't support style sheets, frames, tables, background colours, background images and loads of other things that Web designers take for granted nowadays.

When a browser reads an HTML page, what it is actually doing is 'parsing' (or interpreting) the HTML tags and mapping the page elements as it sees fit. One browser might put a heading in bold, whilst another interprets it in capital letters; emphasised text will be displayed as italics in one browser whilst being emboldened in another; and so on.

So what is a poor Web designer to do? Well, read on and we'll discover many of the answers to this question.

Why bother with the code at all?

It's impossible to open a PC or Internet magazine these days without being bombarded with a plethora of Web-editing programs. Many of these are free, and almost all are very capable beasts in their own right. The industry standard Web editor must surely be Macromedia's Dreamweaver, but Microsoft's FrontPage is a front runner in the 'SoHo' (small office and home) marketplace. Many computer systems come with FrontPage Express already installed. Netscape has its Composer page editor built in to its bulging free Internet suite, while one of our favourite free editors is EvrSoft's 1st Page 2000 which is simply crammed full of gizmos that will do everything for you short of making a cup of coffee.

So given all this software, why should anyone bother with getting their hands dirty with the underlying HTML? The answer is simple. Whilst everything is going smoothly it makes perfect sense to use a commercial editor. But when problems occur (and you can guarantee that problems will occur on each and every Website you create) it is essential to be able to work out why your Web editor is doing what it is doing and how you can get round the problems caused by different browsers interpreting your pages in different ways.

Figure 1.5 There is a wealth of software available to help you build your Web pages.

On top of that there are still many people who firmly believe that coding a page by hand in a text editor such as Notepad is the *only* way to build a proper page. (Others might well describe such techies as 'sad people', but we're certainly not going to get embroiled in this argument!)

A basic page

Let's assume you do use a Web page editor. (Anything to lessen the tedium of hand coding is something we'd welcome.) Why not start by opening up your editor, creating a new blank page and then saving it with nothing added at all.

Not surprisingly, the page displayed in your favourite browser is blank (Figure 1.6) – or it certainly should be!

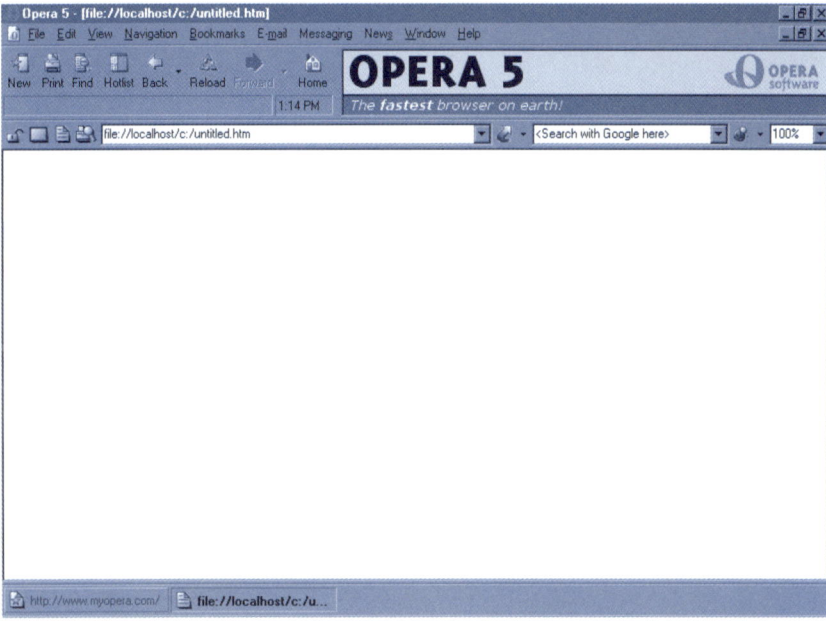

Figure 1.6 As expected, our browser displays a blank page if we have added nothing.

But wait a minute! Switch to the HTML view within your editor and sit back in amazement.

Depending on which Web editor you used you will see that the HTML code is anything but blank. For instance, if you used FrontPage Express you'll see something like:

```
<html>
<head>
<meta http-equiv="Content-Type"
content="text/html; charset=iso-8859-1">
<meta name="GENERATOR" content="Microsoft FrontPage Express 2.0">
<title>Untitled Normal Page</title>
</head>
<body bgcolor="#FFFFFF">
</body>
</html>
```

1st Page will have created:

```
<!DOCTYPE HTML PUBLIC "-//W3C//DTD HTML 4.0 Transitional//EN">
<html>
<head>
```

*Different Web editors switch to the HTML view in different ways, of course. Many, such as Dreamweaver and FrontPage, have tabs that you can use to select between page view and HTML view. Others require you to go to the **View** menu and make your selection. There again, you can also view the HTML code in the browser — for instance, in MS Explorer go to the **View** menu and select **Source**.*

```
<title>Untitled</title>
</head>
<body>
</body>
</html>
```

CoffeeCup will have produced:

```
<html>
<!--   Created with the CoffeeCup HTML Editor   -->
<!--          http://www.coffeecup.com          -->
<!--         Brewed on 9/8/01 6:23:29 PM        -->
<head>
  <title></title>
</head>
<body>
</body>
</html>
```

whilst Dreamweaver will offer you:

```
<html>
<head>
<title>Untitled Document</title>
```

```
<meta http-equiv="Content-Type" content="text/html; charset=
iso-8859-1">
</head>
<body bgcolor="#FFFFFF" text="#000000">
</body>
</html>
```

So what is going on? There seems to be an awful lot of useless stuff in there, which appears to have nothing whatsoever to do with the Web page. To a degree this is so, but we'll revisit these 'useless' bits later in the book. For now, though, let's look at the common elements.

Every page has an `<html>` tag up near the top, closely followed by `<head>`. There then follows a `</head>` tag with `<body>` following on, while at the bottom there's `</body>` followed by `</html>`.

Well, it doesn't take too much brainpower to work out that every tag appears to come in pairs. The whole document is enclosed with `<html>…</html>` and inside that are two pairs: `<head>…</head>` and `<body>…</body>`.

<HTML>

The first page structure tag actually tells your browser that what follows is an HTML document. Everything between the `<html>…</html>` tags is of interest to your browser. Anything that follows can safely be ignored.

All HTML's tags can be written in either UPPER or lower case — it really doesn't matter. They are treated in exactly the same way by your browser. We'll be using both formats in this book to reinforce this point.

`<HEAD>`

Next follows information about the Web page itself. The information here is strictly so that your browser is given some guidance about what is going on. On no account should any textual stuff you want displayed go here.

`<BODY>`

Everything else, including all the material you want displayed in your Web page, should be inserted between the `<body>`...`</body>` tags.

The other stuff

In the codings shown above, there were other lines of extraneous material. What are they for? And does it matter if we remove them? Well, try removing them from your own test page (use a text editor like Notepad to do it) and see what happens. Result? Absolutely nothing! So why have they been inserted?

The answer is that they all do have a purpose, although some are not as obvious as others. Take the opening comments for instance. *1st Page* offered us:

```
<!DOCTYPE HTML PUBLIC "-//W3C//DTD HTML 4.0 Transitional //EN">
```

Because this was contained before the `<HTML>` tag, it is totally ignored by our browsers. (The fact that it is enclosed with `<!` `>` characters shows it to be a comment for information purposes only. We'll return to this in a moment.)

What it tells us is that the code that follows sticks to the World Wide Web Consortium's definitions for HTML version 4 and that it used English as its language. Although this might not be terribly earth-shattering, it might attract more interest if the page characters that follow were in Korean, Chinese or Arabic.

How about CoffeeCup's version that included:

```
<!--     Created with the CoffeeCup HTML Editor     -->
<!--            http://www.coffeecup.com            -->
<!--          Brewed on 9/8/01 6:23:29 PM           -->
```

These lines occur after the `<HTML>` tag but before the `<HEAD>` tag. Again they are enclosed by `<!-- >` symbols and again are totally ignored by the browsers. In effect they are only there so that at a later date you can tell when the pages were created and which editor was used to build them. The URL of CoffeeCup's Website gives the game away that here is a blatant advertisement being stuck into your Web code for others to see. (But there, again, it is a free piece of software, so who are we to complain if they want something in return?)

FrontPage Express and Dreamweaver have both inserted 'Meta' tags such as:

```
<meta name="GENERATOR" content="Microsoft FrontPage Express 2.0">
```

with FPE appearing to use it as an advertisement again. Unlike comments, which can safely be ignored, meta tags do have their uses; in fact when you come to publish your Websites they are absolutely essential. We'll be returning to the subject of meta tags in Chapter 12. Try to contain your impatience until then!

`<TITLE>`

The title tag is used to indicate what your Web page is all about. It is used when your browser displays the page. Try inserting something like:

`<title>pickled aardvark</title>`

into your trial blank page and see how your browser displays it in the top title bar (Figure 1.7).

Figure 1.7 The <TITLE> tag is picked up by your browser.

Obviously you can only have one title in your page, so no other tags should be used in conjunction with it since the words alone are what the browser is looking for. If you add a page to your favourites or hotlist group within your browser, then it will be listed with the title you have given it. It's also useful for people viewing your Website masterpiece to check at a glance that they are at the correct part of your site and haven't clicked their way to somewhere totally different.

A word of warning

We'll end this chapter with a word of caution. Although we have seen that HTML editors are very useful in coding pages for you, you should steer well clear of word processors that offer to do the job of creating Web pages for you. Packages that try to be all things to all people simply do not work.

If you take MS Word as a classic example, you will see exactly what we mean. Try creating a blank page in Word and save it as an HTML page. Now open it up in a text editor and see what it has created for you. ...

```
<html xmlns:o="urn:schemas-microsoft-com:office:office"
xmlns:w="urn:schemas-microsoft-com:office:word"
xmlns="http://www.w3.org/TR/REC-html40">

<head>
<meta http-equiv=Content-Type content="text/html; charset=windows-1252">
<meta name=ProgId content=Word.Document>
<meta name=Generator content="Microsoft Word 9">
<meta name=Originator content="Microsoft Word 9">
<link rel=File-List href="./word_files/filelist.xml">
<!--[if gte mso 9]><xml>
 <o:DocumentProperties>
 <o:Author>Compaq</o:Author>
 <o:LastAuthor>Compaq</o:LastAuthor>
 <o:Revision>1</o:Revision>
 <o:TotalTime>0</o:TotalTime>
 <o:Created>2001-09-08T17:49:00Z</o:Created>
 <o:LastSaved>2001-09-08T17:49:00Z</o:LastSaved>
```

```
  <o:Pages>1</o:Pages>
  <o:Company>Compaq</o:Company>
  <o:Lines>1</o:Lines>
  <o:Paragraphs>1</o:Paragraphs>
  <o:Version>9.2720</o:Version>
 </o:DocumentProperties>
</xml><![endif]-->
<style>
<!--
 /* Style Definitions */
p.MsoNormal, li.MsoNormal, div.MsoNormal
        {mso-style-parent:"";
        margin:0cm;
        margin-bottom:.0001pt;
        mso-pagination:widow-orphan;
        font-size:12.0pt;
        font-family:"Times New Roman";
        mso-fareast-font-family:"Times New Roman";
        mso-ansi-language:EN-GB;}
```

```
@page Section1
    {size:612.0pt 792.0pt;
    margin:72.0pt 90.0pt 72.0pt 90.0pt;
    mso-header-margin:36.0pt;
    mso-footer-margin:36.0pt;
    mso-paper-source:0;}
div.Section1
    {page:Section1;}
-->
</style>
</head>
<body lang=EN-US style='tab-interval:36.0pt'>
<div class=Section1>
<p class=MsoNormal><span lang=EN-GB><![if !supportEmptyParas]
> <![endif]><o:p></o:p></span></p>
</div>
</body>
</html>
```

A blank HTML page whose file size is 1.62 KB? We don't think so!

Text formatting 2

Headings
Paragraphs
Physical styles
Logical styles
Preformatted text
Special characters
Text alignment
Fonts

We ended the last chapter with a whole load of code that MS Word 'kindly' threw into the melting pot of its version of a blank HTML page. We don't need to go into the explanation of that at the moment. But what you will have seen is a whole series of tags that are enclosed in <> brackets.

These tags lie at the heart of successful HTML coding. At their most basic, they can be used for controlling the way page elements look when viewed in a browser. In this chapter we'll be looking at text specifically, and the tags used to alter its appearance.

Headings

Just as you would expect to find in a book, headings are used to divide your pages up into sections. HTML has six levels of heading, with each one being denoted by the letter 'H' followed by a number, enclosed in brackets.

Depending on which browser you are using, your headed text will be displayed bigger, bolder, centred, underlined, capitalised or a combination of some or all of these.

Enclose the text you want as your heading in, for example, `<H1>`...`</H1>` tags – it's common to use H1 as your main 'chapter' heading, with H2 to H6 as sub headings as appropriate.

As an example, type out the following in Notepad and save it as an HTM document such as *headers.htm*. Alternatively, use an HTML editor to add the tags for you (Figure 2.1).

```
<h1>Heading1</h1>
<h2>Heading2</h2>
```

Remember that you can use either upper or lower case letters for your HTML tags. So, <H1> is the same as <h1>. But although tags are not case-sensitive, there are other parts of HTML that are. We'll be seeing where such traps occur later in the book.

```
<h3>Heading3</h3>
<h4>Heading4</h4>
<h5>Heading5</h5>
<h6>Heading6</h6>
```

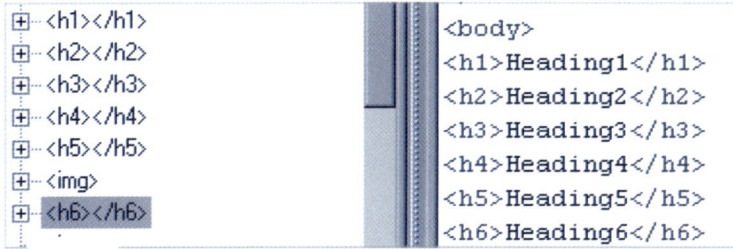

Figure 2.1 CoffeeCup Editor is used to insert the header tags for us.

Remember that it's the browser that decides what your headings will look like. You can only guide it with your header tags to give it the chance of determining the layout of the page in an intelligent way. So, for our example above you shouldn't be surprised to see that Opera and Netscape have both displayed the page using a serif font, whilst Explorer used a sans-serif font (Figure 2.2).

Although they are mainly used for creating visual differentiation on a Web page, headings can also be used to index a page for search engines; so bear this in mind if you have a number of subsections of a document that you want to save in your Web page.

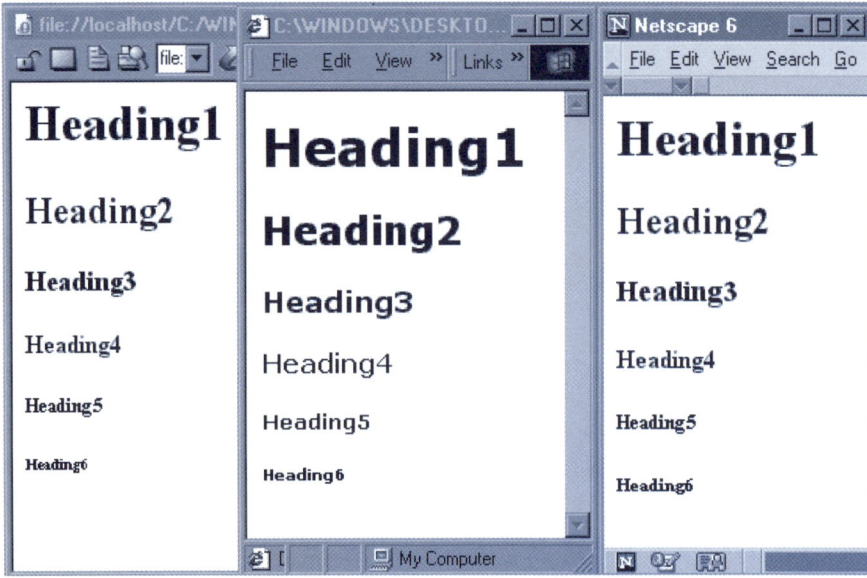

Figure 2.2 Different browsers interpret headers in different ways. Here you can see Opera, IE and Netscape in action.

Paragraphs

One of the main advantages of HTML is that a browser will wrap the text to a new line when it comes to the edge of the screen area (Figure 2.3). If you think about it, that's only sensible since if every browser is going to display text in its own way, it would be impossible to lay out your text for every browser to display properly if it didn't wrap it.

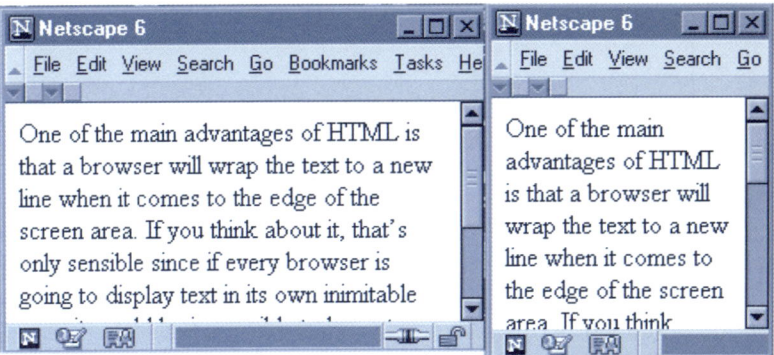

Figure 2.3 As the browser window changes size, the text is wrapped to fit.

This means that, just as in a word processor, you don't need to enter line returns until the end of the paragraph you are working in. In HTML, a paragraph is denoted by the `<P>` tag and this forces the browser to start a new line wherever it is placed.

So if we were to enter the following into our HTML offering:

```
The cat sat on the <p> mat</p>.
```

we would expect to see it laid out in the browser with a line break before the word 'mat' (Figure 2.4).

In earlier specifications of HTML there was no corresponding </P> tag at the end of a paragraph; but from version 4.0 of the HTML specification </P> tags were included. However, the reality is that they make absolutely no difference to your page layout, so it really is up to you whether you choose to use them or not. Some people find it makes their coding easier to follow if they denote the end of a paragraph.

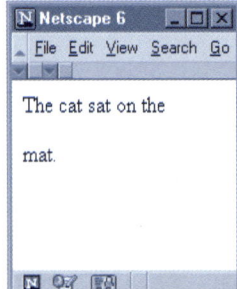

Figure 2.4 A `<P>` tag forces a new line.

Whilst `<P>` is used to denote a new paragraph, you can also force a new line by using the `<BR>` tag. Whenever a browser meets this tag it starts a new line, but unlike `<P>`, it doesn't add extra space above or below it (Figure 2.5).

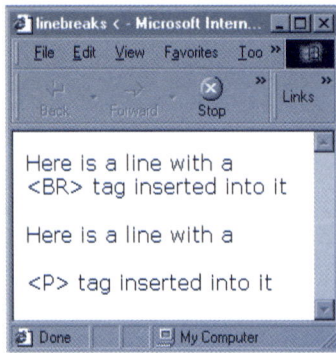

Figure 2.5 A `<BR>` tag doesn't add extra space above or below it.

Physical styles

Tags are very useful for determining the style of text as presented in a browser window. In its earliest form, HTML used only three styles – bold, italic and monospaced. But extra tags have been added with newer iterations of HTML. Here's a roundup of them; most are pretty self explanatory:

`<B>`	Used to **embolden** text.
`<I>`	Makes the enclosed text *italicised*.
`<TT>`	Forces a non-proportional font such as `Courier`.
`<U>`	This tag underlines a word. However, as we shall see in Chapter 5, underlining anything is a bad idea in HTML since this is usually taken to mean that the associated text is hyperlinked.
`<S>`	This is the ~~strikethrough~~ tag, which is discouraged in later versions of HTML.
`<BIG>`	You can use this to make your text bigger.
`<SMALL>`	This tag makes your text smaller.
`<SUB>`	If you want $_{subscript}$, then use this tag.
`<SUP>`	Use this when you want ^{superscript}.

Let's have a look at them in action. Try the following:

```
<b>Bold</b>
<i>Italic</i>
<tt>Monospaced</tt>
```

```
<u>Underlined</u>
<s>Strikethrough</s>
<big>Big</big>
<big><big>Bigger</big></big>
<small>Small</small>
<small><small>Smaller</small></small>
H<sub>2</sub>O
x<sup>2</sup>
```

All being well, you should see something similar to that shown in Figure 2.6.

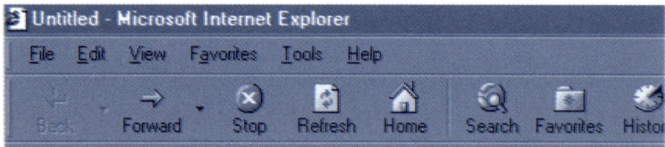

Figure 2.6 Text layout control using simple HTML tags.

Logical styles

The physical styles we have just outlined above are pretty self-explanatory and affect the way that text is displayed in your browser. HTML also has another type of text styling known as *Logical*. These style tags indicate how the highlighted text is to be used, not how it is to be displayed. They could indicate a definition, some program code, or emphasis, for instance, but because you cannot possibly know how any individual browser will display such text, you should not use them for text layout. Many Web designers go through life blissfully ignorant of these tags, and unless you have a particular use for them, you can quite happily forget they ever existed!

In standard HTML there are ten commonly used style tags:

`<ADDRESS>`	Indicates who wrote the Web page and gives author's contact details. Usually placed at the bottom of a page and tends to be italicised.
`<CITE>`	Used to denote a short quotation or citation, and often shows up as italicised text.
`<CODE>`	Denotes a sample of computer code and is often shown in Courier font.
`<DFN>`	A definition which is shown bold or italicised.
`<EM>`	Emphasised text, shown either italicised or bold.
`<KBD>`	Indicates that the text should be typed by the user.
`<BLOCKQUOTE>`	Used for long quotes, unlike the `<CITE>` tag. Often indents the text.

`<SAMP>`	Sample text, similar to `<CODE>`.
`<STRONG>`	A somewhat stronger emphasis than `<EM>`.
`<VAR>`	The name of a variable, often displayed in italic.

Preformatted text

When displaying text in a graphical browser, HTML ignores more than one space between words. In other words,

```
The     cat     sat     on      the     mat
```

is displayed as

```
The cat sat on the mat
```

If you want to keep all your white space, then you should enclose the text within `<PRE>`...`</PRE>` tags. However, all is not as it seems because some browsers will insist on displaying `<PRE>` text in a monospaced font face such as Courier. There are plenty of ways round this, not least using tables and special characters, both of which will be covered later in the book.

If you decide that `<PRE>` tags are for you, then make sure you keep your lines to a maximum of 60 characters, otherwise some of your viewers will have to use the scrollbars to be able to read through your final page.

Special characters

HTML can be pretty restrictive at times. And one thing that it's particularly fussy about is accepting characters that are not normally shown on your keyboard. In general terms, anything such as a © or ® or even characters such as **&**, **#** or { can give problems, and you have to derive them in a different way. Similarly, as we've already noted, spaces of more than one character are totally ignored by HTML.

So what's the secret?

HTML gets round this problem by accepting so-called *named* and *numbered entities*.

- Named entities begin with an ampersand (&) and end with a semicolon (;) and contain an abbreviated name for the character between these two markers.
- Numbered entities have the format: ampersand (&), a hash sign (#), a number and a semicolon (;).

There are loads of named characters, some of which are listed in the Appendix. Numbered characters correspond to the character positions in the ISO-Latin-1 character set used by all word processors. By using a combination of these you can enter foreign characters, mathematical symbols, arrow characters and all kinds of other things.

For example, to write:

```
Schöne Straße
```

we would have to enter

```
Sch&ouml;ne Stra&szlig;e
```

Obviously that can be a bit of a bore, and most Web editors provide an insert-character mechanism whereby you can save yourself some tedious typing (Figure 2.7).

Figure 2.7 1st Page helps you insert special characters.

Text alignment

The vast majority of word processors allow you to range your text either to the right, to the left, centred or justified. HTML is happy to cope with the first three of these. As browsers are going to interpret the content for themselves, there would be little point in having a fully justified tag.

The <ALIGN> tag is used to define text alignment and it contains one of three attributes: **Left**, **Right** or **Center** (note the American spelling).

If you wanted to centre your header, for instance, you could enter:

```
<H1 ALIGN=CENTER>Brian's Ramblings</H1>
```

Or you could right-justify some text:

```
<P ALIGN=RIGHT>Naomi's Peregrinations</P>
```

If you wanted to justify more than one element, it's good form to use the `<DIV></DIV>` pair of tags in the following manner:

```
<H1 ALIGN=CENTER> Trio</H1>
<DIV ALIGN=RIGHT>
<H2>Violin<H2>
<H2>Viola</H2>
<H3>Cello</H3>
</DIV>
```

*You can use `<CENTER>` as a shortened form of `<DIV ALIGN=CENTER>`, although this is not acceptable with the **Left** and **Right** attributes.*

Fonts

The `<FONT>` tag is used in HTML to define the font face, the size of the font and even the colour of the font in use. As we will see later in the book, there are much better ways to define your fonts – namely using style sheets. However, it's necessary to understand how this tag works as it is still found in very many Websites.

There are seven font sizes, with '3' being the default size. So, size 5 is, by definition, two sizes larger than the default.

```
<FONT SIZE=5>Define the font size</FONT>
```

Note that it is up to the browser to define how big or small the text is. The font size is relative to how big the standard size is. Most Web browsers allow you to alter the standard default font size, thus catering for shortsighted people as well as those with excellent vision (Figure 2.8).

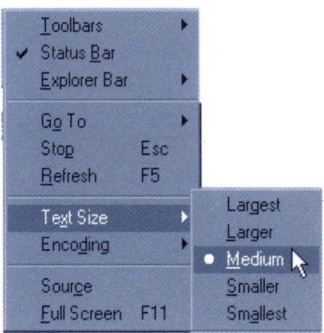

Figure 2.8 MS Explorer allows the viewer to select the default text size.

As well as defining sizes by number, you can also define them in relation to one another (Figure 2.9) such as **–2** or **+3**:

```
Change the <FONT SIZE=+2>Font</FONT> size again
```

Figure 2.9 Different font sizes defined in relationship to one another.

Changing the colour of a font is defined with the `<FONT COLOR>` tag using the hex values used in RGB definitions (we'll be looking at hex values in Chapter 3). For example, the RGB values for red are *255,0,0* which translates into hex as *FF0000*.

So, to create red text you would use:

```
<FONT COLOR="#FF0000">RED</FONT>
```

Graphics, colour and background

3

<IMG> tag
Aligning text with images
Controlling text wrapping
Image spacing
Image scaling
Image previews
Image alternatives
Background images
Background colours
Horizontal rules

We all know that a picture is worth a thousand words, and a Website without an `<IMG>` tag would be a boring site indeed.

Images on Websites can be in one of three formats, although the vast majority are in one of the first two:

- **GIF**   The *Graphical Image Format* is used for clip art and pictures where vast areas use the same colour. Because the coding defines areas of like colour, GIF pictures can compress the information very effectively and produce files of a small size. The maximum number of colours in a GIF image is only 256, which means that GIFs are not really suitable for photographs; however, with a little bit of tweaking you can get reasonably good quality pictures using GIFs.
- **JPEG**   The *Joint Photographic Experts Group* defined this format for pictures with large numbers of colours and gradients. JPEGs use what is known as a lossy compression format – which means that the more you compress your file, the worse the quality of the picture becomes. The trick is to squeeze the file as far as you can go without any discernible loss of quality; and often this will allow you to more than halve the file size before any visible damage is done to the picture.
- **PNG**   *Ping* files, as they are known – or *Portable Network Graphics* files – were proposed as a replacement for GIFs. Although a number of professional graphics programs allow one to save files in PNG format, they are still (at the time of writing) something of a rarity on the Web.

Because no one wants a Web page to take forever and a day to load just because you happen to have used a large graphic on it, you really should – if you haven't already – learn how to 'optimise' both JPEG and GIF files to make them as small as possible. There are many imaging programs that allow you to do this (Figure 3.1), most notably:

3: Graphics, colour and background

- Photoshop
- Fireworks
- Paint Shop Pro
- Image Optimizer

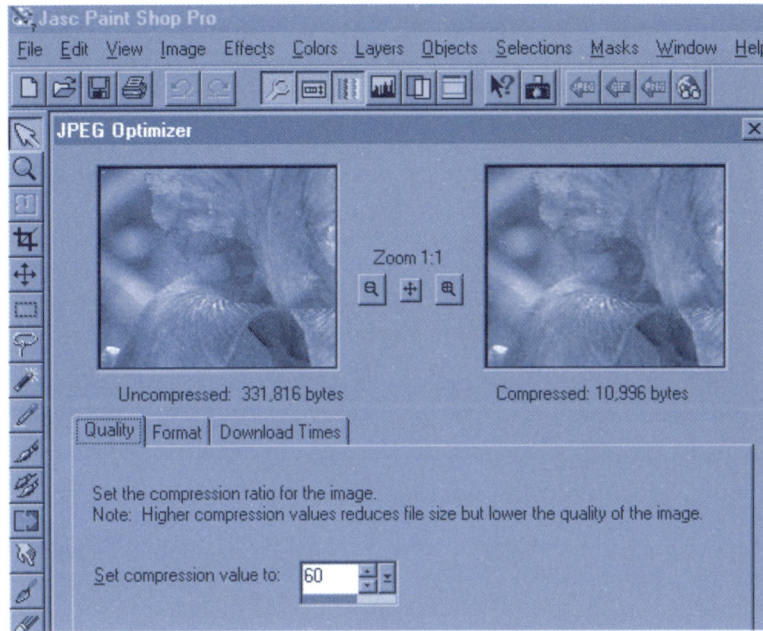

Figure 3.1 Paint Shop Pro is excellent at reducing the size of Web graphics.

`<IMG>` tag

In order to place graphics onto your Web page, you'll need to use the `<IMG>` tag. This tag has no closing tag (such as `</IMG>`) but can come with many attributes, the most important of which is **SRC**.

SRC denotes the source filename, or URL, where the browser can find the image file. Since it is best, wherever possible, to use relative path names, rather than absolute path names, you can use ../ to denote a directory one up from the current directory, ../../ for a directory two up from the current directory and so on.

So, if you have a file whose name is *image.gif* in a folder called *images*, and the Web page is in the base directory, your image tag might look like:

```
<IMG SRC="images/image.gif">
```

On the other hand, if image.gif was in the images folder, whilst the Web page was in a folder called *pages* which was one level down from the base directory, then your image tag might look like:

```
<IMG SRC="../images/image.gif">
```

Let's add a picture to a Web page. First insert a title, and follow that up with a heading for your page. Now add an image, and your HTML code should resemble this:

```
<html>
<head>
<title>Flowers I have known and loved</title>
```

Image filenames are case-sensitive on some servers (notably UNIX), so get into the habit of making your filenames all lower case.

```
</head>
<H1>Flowers I have known and loved</H1><img src="plant.jpg">
</body>
</html>
```

The first thing you'll notice, when you view the Web page in your browser, is that the image is placed on a line after the heading (Figure 3.2).

Figure 3.2 The image is displayed on a separate line from the heading.

But what happens if you want the heading to run alongside the picture? Simply place the image tag *inside* the header tags (Figure 3.3), thus:

```
<H3><img src="plant.jpg">Flowers I have known and loved</H3>
```

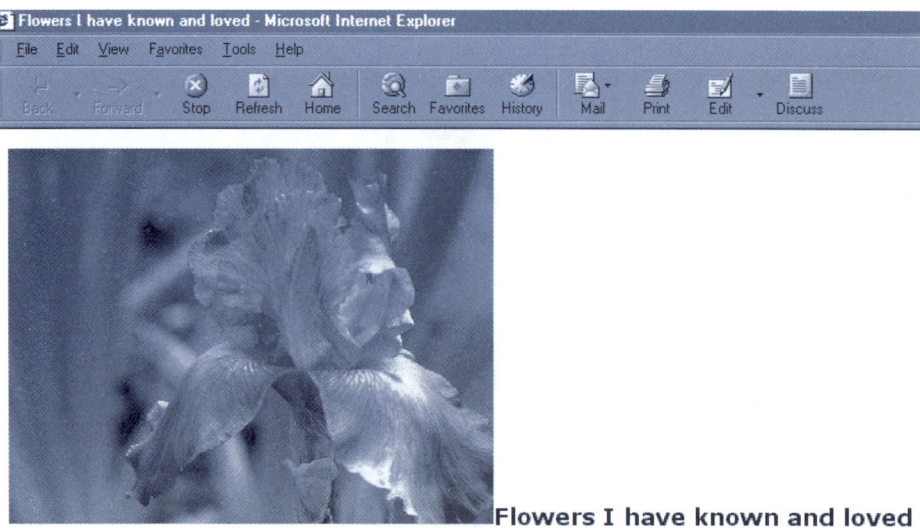

Figure 3.3 Here we can force the header to be on the same line as the image.

Of course, you could use an image anywhere in a block of text – not just at either end of it. Consider:

```
<html>
<head>
</head>
<H3>Flags of the world</H3>
<p>Egypt <IMG SRC="egypt.jpg"> Israel <IMG SRC="israel.jpg">
Saudi <IMG SRC="saudi.jpg"></p>
</body>
</html>
```

Here the text and images are all enclosed within a paragraph, and the result is that both the images and the text are aligned in relation to the bottom of the text (Figure 3.4).

Figure 3.4 Images can be placed in the middle of a line of text.

Aligning text with images

This last example might not be what you had wanted. After all, not everyone wants things lined up along the bottom. So those wise inventors of HTML decided to incorporate some more attributes into the `<IMG>` tag – namely:

- **Align=Top**
- **Align=Middle**
- **Align=Bottom**

These attributes allow you to align everything to the topmost part of the line (which might include other images or just text, depending on what is there), or the centre of the image with the middle of the line, or the bottom of the image with the bottom of the line (Figure 3.5). So your code might read:

```
<H3>Flags of the world</H3>
<P>Egypt <IMG SRC="egypt.jpg" Align="Top"> </P>
<P>Israel <IMG SRC="israel.jpg" Align="Middle"> </P>
<P>Saudi <IMG SRC="saudi.jpg" Align="Bottom"></P>
```

There are more alignment attributes which are not officially part of the HTML definition, but which are commonly found, nonetheless:

Align=TextTop　Here, the top of the image is aligned with the top of the tallest text, rather than the top of the tallest item, in the line.

Align=AbsMiddle　Aligns the middle of the image with the middle of the largest item on the line.

Align=Baseline   The same as Align=Bottom.

Align=AbsBottom Aligns the bottom of the image with the lowest item in the line (which isn't necessarily the text).

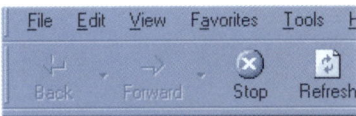

Figure 3.5 Aligning text at the top, middle and bottom of the images.

Controlling text wrapping

And just when you thought it was safe to raise your head above the parapet, yet more `<IMG>` attributes want to make themselves known.

If you wish to wrap multiple lines round an image, you can't just place the image within the line of text and hope it will wrap around by magic. Unfortunately, the text and the image make up one line, so any excess text means it will start a new line under the image. This isn't necessarily what you want.

Enter two more attributes:

- **Align="Left"**
- **Align="Right"**

Now, any text you enter following one of these little beauties is wrapped around until it runs out of space (Figure 3.6):

Figure 3.6 Using Align="Left" to wrap round a picture.

```
<IMG SRC="flower.jpg" Align="Left">
<H2>Peter Piper Picked a Peck of Pickled Pepper;<Br>
```

```
A Peck of Pickled Pepper Peter Piper Picked;<Br>
If Peter Piper Picked that Peck of Pickled Pepper;<Br>
Where's the Peck of Pickled Pepper Peter Piper Picked?</h2>
```

You'll have noticed that simply inserting a `<BR>` or `<P>` tag doesn't stop the text from wrapping. For that you'll need yet another series of attributes:

- **Clear="Left"**
- **Clear="Right"**
- **Clear="All"**

Try adding a `<CLEAR>` tag to the code and see the resultant line split (Figure 3.7).

Figure 3.7 Using the `<CLEAR>` tag to break the text wrap.

```
<IMG SRC="flower.jpg" Align="Left">
<H2>Peter Piper Picked a Peck of Pickled Pepper;<BR Clear="Left">
A Peck of Pickled Pepper Peter Piper Picked;<Br>
If Peter Piper Picked that Peck of Pickled Pepper;<Br>
Where's the Peck of Pickled Pepper Peter Piper Picked?</h2>
```

Image spacing

Since you can now wrap text around an image, you will almost certainly want to clear some space around it so that it doesn't look crowded.

`<VSPACE>` and `<HSPACE>` allow you to determine the space in pixels above and below, and to the left and right of the image respectively. An example should suffice to illustrate what we mean. In the following code, the text wraps to the right of the image (Figure 3.8).

```
<IMG SRC="lynx.jpg" Align="Left">
Amongst your peregrinations through the African bush,
you might be lucky enough to see a lynx, assuming, that is,
that you're not too forjeskit.
```

Whereas in the next bit of code, a border of 50 pixels is thrown around the image, pushing the text away and leaving plenty of white space (Figure 3.9).

3: Graphics, colour and background

Figure 3.8 Here the text wraps closely to the image.

Figure 3.9 Using `<VSPACE>` and `<HSPACE>` to add white space.

```
<IMG SRC="lynx.jpg" VSpace=50 HSpace=50 Align="Left">
Amongst your peregrinations through the African bush,
you might be lucky enough to see a lynx, assuming, that is,
that you're not too forjeskit.
```

Image scaling

Two more `<IMG>` attributes are used to scale the size of your images, and these are

- **Height**
- **Width**

You could argue that it would be worth scaling your images first so that they are the correct size for what you need. But this misses the point. What if you use an image more than once – in which case the first time the image is used, it will be loaded into the browser's cache and load up much faster next time. And you may want to tweak it just a little to fit your page. In which case use the tags like this, where the numbers given are the values in pixels:

```
<IMG SRC="lynx.jpg" width="384" height="288">
```

Image previews

One thing which is almost guaranteed to irritate your Web visitors is having to wait a long time for a large image to appear on one of your pages. Wouldn't it be convenient if a low-resolution image could first appear whilst the higher resolution image loads in the background so that there is something for the visitor to look at almost straight away?

Well, those HTML gurus thought so too, and they came up with the `<LOWSRC>` tag to allow you to do just that.

Let's assume you have a lower resolution version of *image.jpg* called *imagelow.jpg* which you have prepared with your favourite image processor (we saw earlier on how you can determine the compression of a JPEG file).

Now, if you type in:

```
<IMG SRC = "image.jpg" LOWSRC = "imagelow.jpg">
```

your browser will load the low-resolution image on its first pass, and then when all the layout has been loaded, it will have another go, this time loading the better quality image.

Image alternatives

It's easy to forget these days where new versions of Web browsers appear to come out on an almost monthly basis that some people still use text-only browsers, or choose to turn their graphics off to help speed up page downloading.

Using the `ALT` attribute to the `<IMG>` tag you can supply some alternative text, which not only provides a textual clue as to what the image is all about, but in some browsers also comes up with a prompt when your cursor hovers over the image.

Try something along the following lines in your HTML:

```
<IMG SRC = "lynx.jpg" ALT = "this is a lynx">
```

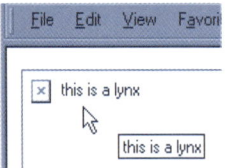

Figure 3.10 An ALT attribute provides a textual clue as to what the image is all about.

Background images

We've seen how to load images into your Web pages, but it may well be that you want to have an image permanently in the background. This is where the BACKGROUND attribute is brought in as part of the <BODY> tag.

When you use an image as a background, it tiles itself across and down the page to fill the browser window (Figure 3.11).

Figure 3.11 Background images tile across the browser window.

When you have a background image, it scrolls up the page as you scroll your browser window. However, later browsers can deal with what is known as a **watermark**. By inserting

```
BGPROPERTIES=FIXED
```

into the `<BODY BACKGROUND>` tag, you can anchor the background so that it doesn't move.

Background colours

While we're on the subject of backgrounds, you can always decide to have a plain coloured background. Changing background colour is simply a matter of using the `BGCOLOR` attribute within the `<BODY>` tag. You can use either hex values or the name of the colour. So, for instance:

```
<BODY BGCOLOR = "#FF0000">
```

is the same as

```
<BODY BGCOLOR = red>
```

Not all browsers support named colours, so it's usually better to use the hex value if at all possible. However, if you're interested, we have included a table of all the equivalent colours with their hex values in the Appendix.

Horizontal rules

It's quite neat to be able to have a horizontal rule-off on your pages when you're wanting to separate blocks of text or underscore a heading, for example. HTML provides a very easy way to do this without having to go to all the trouble of making an image file containing a single solid line.

The `<HR>` tag does just this. There is no closing tag associated with it, nor any text; but you can have various attributes added to give you extra control over its look and feel. Specifically, these attributes are:

- **Size**
- **Width**
- **Align**

The **Size** attribute is a measure of thickness of the line given in pixels. The thinnest line you can create is 2 pixels, and this is also the default if you don't specify what you want. Figure 3.12 shows what the following code will produce:

```
<html>
<head>
<title>Rule offs</title>
</head>
<body bgcolor="#FFFFFF">
<hr size = "2">2 pixels
<hr size = "4">4 pixels
<hr size = "8">8 pixels
<hr size = "12">12 pixels
<hr size = "16">16 pixels
</body>
</html>
```

3: Graphics, colour and background

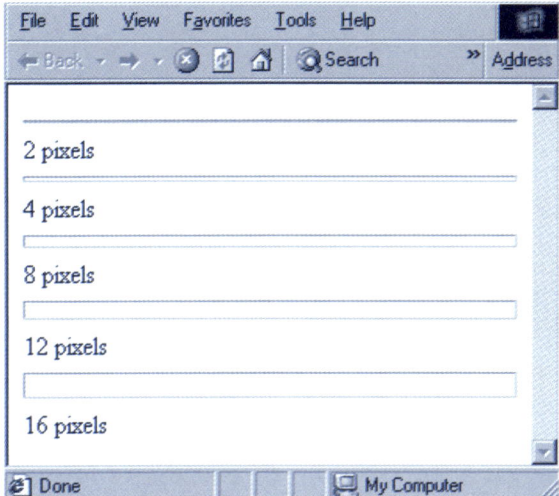

Figure 3.12 Varying line widths using the `<HR>` tag.

As well as the thickness of the line, you can also specify the width of the line across the Web page. Although you can specify an exact length in pixels, it is more usual to give a measurement as a percentage of the page width. Figure 3.13 shows what the code below will produce:

```
<html>
<head>
<title>Rule offs</title>
</head>
```

54 HTML

```
<body bgcolor="#FFFFFF">
<hr width="75%">75 percent
<hr width ="50%">50 percent
<hr width ="25%">25 percent
<hr width="50">50 pixels
</body>
</html>
```

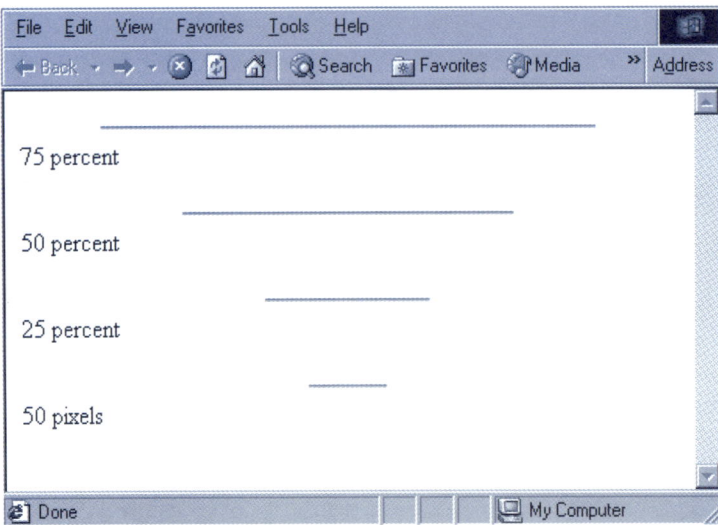

Figure 3.13 Varying line lengths using the Width attribute.

If the width of the line is specified as smaller than the width of the actual screen, then it possible to determine the alignment of the line:

- **Left**
- **Right**
- **Center**

By default, lines are shown centred, but here is some code to give us a variety (Figure 3.14):

```
<html>
<head>
<title>Rule offs</title>
</head>
<body bgcolor="#FFFFFF">
<hr width="75%" align="left"><p>
<hr width ="75%" alignn="center"><p>
<hr width ="75%" align="right"><p>
</body>
</html>
```

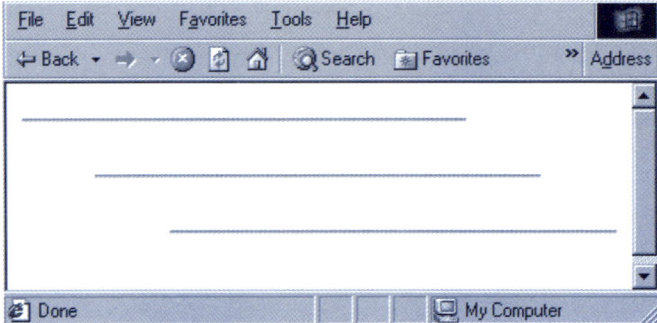

Figure 3.14 Adjusting the alignment of horizontal rules.

Multimedia 4

Sound

Video

Flash and Shockwave

Java applets

As well as the inclusion of text and images in your Website, the ever-growing speed of the Internet, combined with newer delivery mechanisms such as cable, ADSL and short-range radio links, has meant that multimedia has finally come of age on the Internet.

Sound and video files are now commonly embedded into Websites, as are other types of multimedia files, including:

- MP3 and other sound files
- QuickTime and other video formats
- Flash and Shockwave
- Java applets.

Sound

There are several different types of sound files and formats, and several different ways to add sound to a Web page. Some factors to consider before deciding on a format and method for adding sound are its purpose, your audience, file size, sound quality and differences in browsers.

Linking to an audio file is a simple and effective way to add sound to a Web page, allowing visitors to choose whether they want to listen to the file in the first place without necessarily downloading it first. (As sound files can be fairly large in size, your visitors might not be happy if you force them to download something they are not interested in!)

If you are sure you want to embed the sound file into your Web page, you have first to ensure that your visitors have the correct plug-in to allow them to listen to it. You'll need to embed files if you want to use the sound as background music, or if you want more control over the sound presentation itself. (For example, you can set the volume, the way the player looks on the page, and the beginning and ending points of the sound file.)

As we've said, there are plenty of different sound file formats around, but the most common ones are:

.midi or .mid	**Musical Instrument Digital Interface**	MIDI files are supported by many browsers and don't require a plugin. Although their sound quality is very good, it can vary depending on a visitor's sound card. A small MIDI file can provide a long sound clip. MIDI files cannot be recorded and must be synthesised on a computer with special hardware and software.
.wav	**Waveform Extension**	These have good sound quality, are supported by many browsers, and don't require a plugin. You can record your own WAV files from a CD, tape, microphone, and so on. However, the large file size severely limits the length of sound clips that you can use on your Web pages.
.aif	**Audio Interchange File Format, or AIFF**	AIFF files, like WAV format, have good sound quality, can be played by most browsers, and don't require a plugin; you can also record AIFF files from a CD, tape, micro-phone, and so on. However, the large file size severely limits the length of sound clips that you can use on your Web pages.

.mp3	**Motion Picture Experts Group Audio Layer-3**	A compressed format that makes sound files substantially smaller. The sound quality is very good: if an MP3 file is recorded and compressed properly, its quality can rival that of a CD. The file can be 'streamed' so that a visitor doesn't have to wait for the entire file to download before hearing it. However, the file size is larger than a Real Audio file, so a whole song could still take quite a while to download over a normal phone line connection. To play MP3 files, visitors must download and install a plugin such as QuickTime, Windows Media Player or RealPlayer.
.ra, .ram, .rpm	**Real Audio**	Has a very high degree of compression with smaller file sizes than MP3. Whole song files can be downloaded in a reasonable amount of time. Because the files can be 'streamed' from a normal Web server, visitors can begin listening to the sound before the file has completely downloaded. The sound quality is poorer than that of MP3 files, but new players and encoders have improved quality considerably. Visitors must download and install the RealPlayer plugin in order to play these files (Figure 4.1).

4: Multimedia

You can link to a sound file in the normal way. For instance:

```
<P>The Beatles' <A HREF="erigby.wav">Eleanor Rigby</A> has
a great cello solo</P>
```

but you might prefer instead to have the song play whilst the page is being viewed. If so, you should use the `<BGSOUND...>` tag.

The HTML used to insert a background sound into a page is:

```
<BGSOUND SRC="erigby.wav">
```

With `<BGSOUND>` you have the choice of setting a number of attributes:

BALANCE= Stereo balancing The BALANCE attribute can be used to change the stereo balance when the sound file is played. It accepts values between '–10 000' and '10 000'. The effect of the two extreme values depends on the sound settings on the users system, but using either of the extreme values will force the sound to play from one speaker only.

LOOP=n This attribute specifies how many times a sound will loop when activated. If n=–1 or LOOP=INFINITE is specified, the sound will loop indefinitely.

SRC This specifies the address of a sound to be played.

Be wary of having sounds play whenever a page loads. For those with slower connections the page could take an absolute age to download and you will probably end up annoying your visitors.

VOLUME=n   The VOLUME attribute accepts values between '–10 000' and '0' and can be used to set the volume at which the sound file will play. Note that using '0' (i.e. maximum volume) will play the sound file at 100% of the user's current volume settings. There is no way in HTML that you can force a sound file to play at a volume indecent to the user. They will always have total control!

Figure 4.1 RealPlayer can cope with a wide variety of audio and video formats.

Video

Just as with sound, there are a number of video file formats, the most common of which are:

.avi	**Audio Video Interleave**	Microsoft's Video for Windows standard.
.mov	**QuickTime**	Apple's QuickTime originated on Mac computers but was soon ported to PCs as well.
.mpeg, .mpg	**Motion Picture Experts Group**	The universal standard across the Web with files typically smaller than those of either the above two standards.

Once again, the HTML code is quite straightforward:

```
<A HREF="brian.mpg">A video of Brian, self-effacing as ever!
(2MB) </A>
```

Flash and Shockwave

Macromedia's Flash technology has become a standard for the delivery of vector-based graphics and animations on the Web, whilst Shockwave is Macromedia's standard for interactive multimedia on the Web. Browsers need to have a Flash Player or Shockwave plug-in to be able to run such content, but most browsers now include these as standard, since these files are ubiquitous across the Web.

Note that with video files, especially, it is helpful for your visitors to be told how big a file they are being asked to download, since those with slower connections will not otherwise know what they are letting themselves in for in terms of download time.

When you insert a Flash movie into a document, you need to use both the **object** tag (defined by Internet Explorer for ActiveX controls) and the **embed** tag (defined by Netscape Navigator) to get the best results in all browsers.

```
<OBJECT classid="clsid:D27CDB6E-AE6D-11cf-96B8-444553540000"
codebase=http://download.macromedia.com/pub/shockwave/cabs
/flash/swflash.cab#version=5,0,0,0 WIDTH=550 HEIGHT=400>
<PARAM NAME=movie VALUE="Movie1.swf">
<PARAM NAME=quality VALUE=best>
<PARAM NAME=bgcolor VALUE=#FFFFFF>
<EMBED   src="Movie1.swf"   quality=best   bgcolor=#FFFFFF
WIDTH=550 HEIGHT=400 TYPE="application/x-shockwave-flash"
PLUGINSPAGE="http://www.macromedia.com/shockwave/down-
load/index.cgi?P1_Prod_Version=ShockwaveFlash"></EMBED>
</OBJECT>
```

This probably looks hugely complicated; but whichever program you use to create your Flash or Shockwave movies, you'll find it 'publishes' the code for you and all you have to do is copy and paste it into your Web page.

Java applets

You can use Java applets to react to your visitors' input without having to check back to the server each time, as you would need to do with ordinary forms (see Chapter 10). But they can also be used for a wide variety of effects and animations, though in general they take longer to load into a browser than other multimedia files such as Flash (Figure 4.2).

4: Multimedia

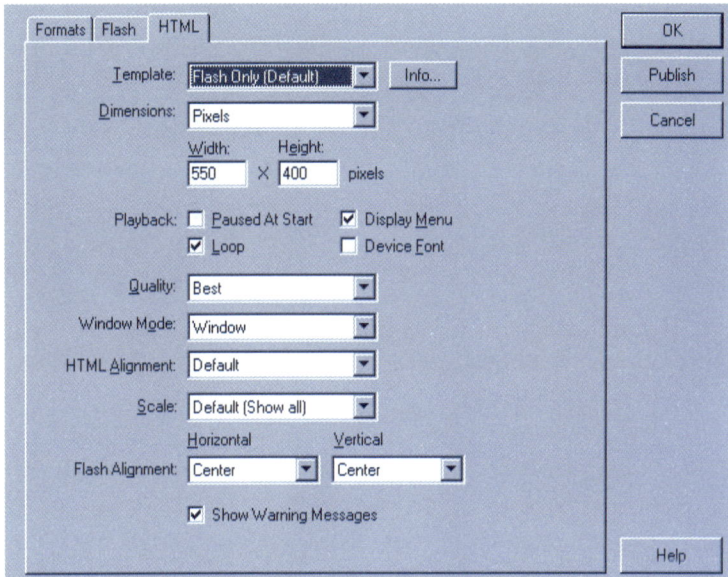

Figure 4.2 Macromedia's Flash works out all the HTML coding for you.

There are plenty of Java applet programs that you can download from the Web or insert directly from Web editor programs, and all you have to do is insert a small amount of HTML on your page to enable them to be displayed.

Java applets have their program code defined in class files, which need to be stored in the same directory as the Web page. Any parameters which change certain elements within the Java applet are then inserted after the class definition within the HTML; for those without Java capability (or for those who have Java 'switched off') you can add an alternative image for the browser to display:

```
<applet code="MyApplet.class" width=150 height=150>
<param name=param1 value="1234">
<param name=param2 value="5678">
<IMG ALT="alternate text" ALIGN=center SRC="alternateimage.gif" border=0>
</applet>
```

Don't worry, though. If you have got as far as finding a Java applet to download off the Internet, the chances are almost 100% that instructions for embedding it within your HTML will come with it!

Links and image maps

5

HREF
Relative path names
Absolute path names
Linking to Web pages
Linking to specific locations
Special characters
Mailto:
Using images as links
Image maps

One of the most important elements – nay, the *most* important element – of HTML is the hypertext properties it can provide to allow your user to jump from one page element to another, either within the same Website, or to another totally unrelated part of the Internet.

The **Link Tag** which manages this is also known as an **Anchor Tag** and is represented by `<A>...</A>`

The Link tag always comes with attributes since it simply would make no sense for the `<A>` tag to exist on its own. Let's see why.

HREF

The most common attribute is **HREF**, which is short for **H**ypertext **Ref**erence. This is used to point to the name or URL of the file or page in question. All text between the opening and closing `<A>` tags will act as a hyperlink and will (normally) be highlighted in some way – whether it is underlined, coloured differently, emboldened, or whatever.

Say you wanted to link to, and call up, a page which is stored in the same folder or directory in which your current page is stored. A typical link might look like:

```
<A HREF = "page2.htm"> Click here to go to page 2 </A>
```

For instance, we might have a page that refers to a firm of solicitors. By creating a link tag and attaching it to the name of the firm, we should be able to allow our users to jump straight to another page for more information (Figure 5.1).

```
<H1> Professional Firms in Yorkshire </H1>
<P>Harrogate is home to many well-known legal firms, the
```

5: Links and image maps

```
most famous of which is <A HREF = "bashforth.htm">Bashforth
and Strumpet</A>, conveniently located in Kent Road.</P>
```

Figure 5.1 Here, the hyperlink is indicated by underlined text.

Relative path names

We've seen how easy it is to link to pages contained in the same directory or folder on your hard drive or local Website.

Remember that file names are case-sensitive. Although your browser might be perfectly capable of finding a filename in upper case when you have specified it in lower case, you will almost certainly come to grief when your Website is uploaded to a UNIX server. This is NOT the case with HTML tags which are not case-sensitive and where you could (if you really wanted to) mix, say, <A> with </a>.

Folders and directories are two words which really mean the same thing. But Windows, Mac, Unix, DOS and RISC OS users all have their favourites. We'll use them interchangeably in this book.

If you feel you need to specify a drive letter on your hard disk as part of your relative path name, then instead of using c:/ or d:/ or whatever, you use the 'pipe' character instead of the colon, thus: c|/

The browser simply takes a reference to another HTML file (or page) as a relative path from the original file. But, of course, in real life you're likely to want to point to links contained in other directories and here the way to let the browser 'find' your new file is to specify it using UNIX-type path names.

Let's give a couple of examples to make it clear.

If our original (home) page is located in the base directory, then if we wish to point to a second page contained in a subfolder called *files2*, we would refer to it as:

    HREF = "files2/page2.htm"

But if a third page was sitting comfortably in a directory called *files3*, which was itself sitting within *files2*, we would instead refer to it as:

    HREF = "files2/files3/page3.htm"

Similarly, if we wanted a hyperlink from page 3 to point to page 2 we would insert:

    HREF = "../page2.htm

whilst if we wanted to point to the first page from page 3 the reference would look like:

    HREF = "../../page1.htm

Absolute path names

Sometimes it makes better sense when specifying a link to another page to use an **Absolute** path name. Remember:

- **Relative** path names describe links relative to the page you are on at the time.
- **Absolute** path names describe links relative to the top level of the directory structure.

You can tell an absolute path name a mile off. Every one starts with a forward slash (/) followed by all the directories in the path from the top down to where the file is located. Hence,

```
HREF = "/c|/files/morefiles/yetmorefiles/file.htm"
```

would refer to *file.htm* located on the *c:* drive in directories *files/morefiles/yetmorefiles*.

Linking to Web pages

It's all very well linking to pages on your hard drive, or on a local network, but the majority of hyperlinks refer to other pages located somewhere on the Internet. Setting up hyperlinks to Web pages is probably even easier than specifying absolute path names. Instead of the file path, you simply insert the URL, or address, of the page in question.

Say that you want to make a link from one of your pages to the home page on Topspin Group. Its URL is www.topspin-group.com. Let's assume the home page is called *index.htm*. So to make a hyperlink to this home page would look something like:

```
<A HREF = "http://www.topspin-group.com/index.htm"> Topspin Home Page</A>
```

Most browsers display the URL of the page you are currently visiting, so if you want to create a hyperlink to this particular page, simply copy and paste this URL into your <A> tags and save yourself the typing!

Linking to specific locations

It's all very well to link to another page, but it could be that the linked-to page is either very long, or full of text and will involve your readers having to scroll down the page in search of the particular piece if information you want them to find.

You can get round this problem by using bookmarks, or 'anchors', within the linked-to page and referring to them in your hyperlinks.

Anchors are created in exactly the same way in HTML – i.e. by use of the <A> tag. But instead of using HREF, you use the **NAME** attribute. This takes one or more keywords to identify the anchor and when you jump to this location, these keywords are placed at the top of the browser window (Figure 5.2).

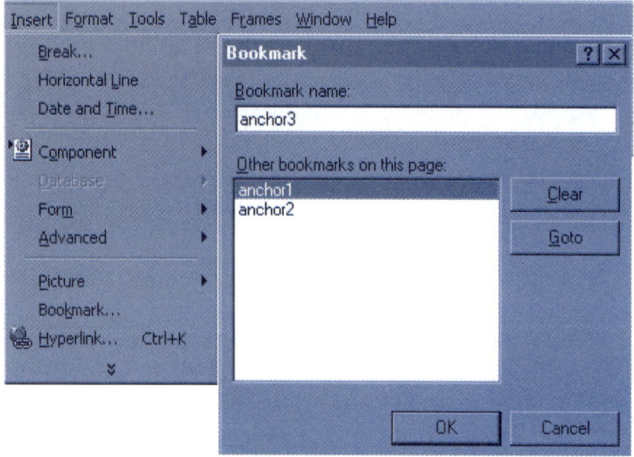

Figure 5.2 Some Web editors such as FrontPage refer to 'bookmarks' when inserting anchor tags.

So, if you were writing your memoirs and had decided to inflict them on the general public, you might name one section *The Teenage Years*. You would probably want to format this as a heading and, more specifically, you could give it an anchor so that hyperlinks can refer directly to it:

```
<H1><A NAME = "teenage">The Teenage Years</A></H1>
```

In this example the word 'teenage' is our named attribute, so we could point to the Web page in question (*memoirs.htm*) and then specifically refer to this anchor by using a hash (#) sign:

```
<A HREF = "memoirs.htm#teenage">Click here to read about me as a teenager</A>
```

You don't actually need to jump to another page to use anchors. After all, if you have a large page, it is often rather useful to be able to jump around within the page itself. To link to these anchors, simply use the anchor name with its hash sign and some text to identify the hyperlink:

```
Go to <A HREF = "#teenage">The Teenage Years</A>
```

Special characters

Sometimes you might need to insert some special character into a URL in order to allow every type of browser to understand it. For instance, if you had created a directory called *My Files* within your directory structure, some browsers would fall over if you typed in a URL such as:

```
www.website/My Files/index.htm
```

Unlike links, anchors are invisible on a viewed Web page. It's only when you jump to them that you know they are there!

Browsers aren't too crazy about having spaces in URLs, just as they'd really rather you didn't use question marks. Instead they'd be much happier if you entered escape codes which are represented by a percentage sign (%) followed by a two-character hex symbol from the ISO-Latin-1 character set. For instance, a space is denoted by *%20*, whilst a question mark is *%2f*.

So our URL would now look like:

```
www.website/My%20Files/index.htm
```

The best advice is to keep things simple and to try to avoid spaces and other characters that screw up your URLs.

Mailto:

Not only can you link to another Web page, but HTML can also be used to send electronic mail automatically via a hyperlink.

To create a hyperlink on a page so that any visitor who clicks on it can automatically have your email address appear in their email client and prompt them for a subject and the body of their message, use:

```
<A HREF = "mailto:brian@topspin-group.com">Brian</A>
```

where your email address is placed after **mailto:**.

Many Web editors will insert the correct syntax for a *mailto:* command automatically (Figure 5.3), but – there again – many don't!

5: Links and image maps

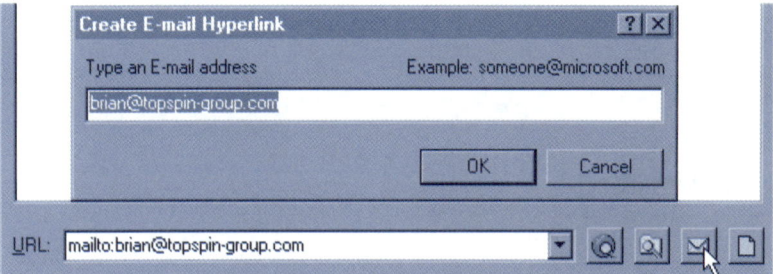

Figure 5.3 FrontPage helps you to get syntax correct in a Mailto: command.

Using images as links

There's no reason at all why you cannot use images as links, rather than text. In fact, your Web pages might look very dull if you didn't use image links.

You can actually use both text and images within the same <A> ... </A> tags so that both image and text can point to another location. Consider:

```
<A HREF = "birds.htm" ><IMG SRC = "eagle.gif">Our feathered
friends</A>
```

By default, images that are used as 'hotspots' for links have borders around them to make then stand out from other images. However, many people prefer to have these borders switched off (Figure 5.4) since hovering over the image will normally show up a hotspot anyway, and they can make your Web page look pretty ugly!

To switch off the hotspot border, insert a **Border** attribute into the `<IMG>` tag so that:

```
Border = 0.
```

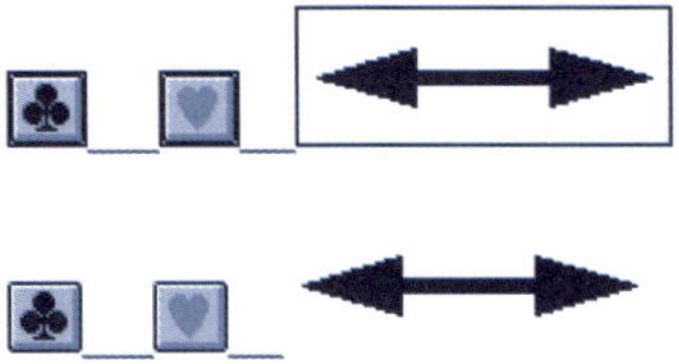

Figure 5.4 Image hotspots normally have borders (above) but these can be turned off (below).

Image maps

There are many instances when it is better not to have a hyperlink represented by an entire picture, but rather by an area within a picture. For instance, if you had a map of Europe, you might want your users to click on the UK to have an English language Web page appear, Dutch if you clicked on Holland, Catalan if you clicked on Andorra, and so on.

Image maps are used to activate different parts of an image to make local hotspots to take the visitor to different areas of your Website, pertinent to the area of the picture he clicked on.

There are two types of image map:

- **Server-Side**
- **Client-Side.**

The former were used in the early days of the Web, but caused many problems – associated with the server used for hosting the Website. It was necessary to run a special program on the server itself in order to tell the browser what each click coordinate meant. Instead, client-side maps use the visitor's browser to decode the information, and are the preferred method for creating such maps.

There are many image mapping programs available, and for something as complicated as this it would hardly be sensible to try to work out all the coordinates by hand. Nevertheless, it makes sense to understand what is going on so that, if nothing else, you can still tweak the settings the way you want them to look.

The heart of the image map is a tag called, simply, `<MAP>`. Its format looks something like:

```
<MAP NAME = "example"> coordinates and links </MAP>
```

The coordinates for the hotspots on your image can be calculated by your image mapping program, or you can work them out for yourself, if you are up to the task. Immediately following the coordinates is an HREF attribute to tell the browser where to link.

The coordinates are included within another tag: `<AREA>`. This tag has an attribute called **SHAPE** and shapes can be rectangles (RECT), circles (CIRCLE) and polygons (POLY).

So, a polygon might have an AREA tag using combinations of x and y values such as:

```
<area shape = "poly" coords="x_1,y_1,x_2,y_2,x_3,y_3,x_4,y_4" href= "example.htm">
```

Figure 5.5 Hotspot areas can be laid over an image.

Working out rectangular coordinates is easy enough. The upper left hand corner of the rectangle is denoted by x_1, y_1, whilst the bottom right corner has the coordinates x_2, y_2. For instance, the three rectangles shown in Figure 5.5 might have <AREA> tags such as:

```
<area shape="rect" coords="75,134,152,204" href="example1.htm" >

<area shape="rect" coords="165,81,251,158" href="example2.htm" >

<area shape="rect" coords="51,43,126,107" href="example3.htm" >
```

Circles are denoted by x,y coordinates for the centre of the circle with a radius of z. So:

```
<area shape="circle" coords="x,y,z" href="example.htm">
```

In the same way that you can use ALT tags with images (see Chapter 3) you can use them with image maps to bring up a short description of the mapped area when you hover your cursor over it.

Once you have defined your coordinates and your image map using the `<MAP>` tag, you then need to place the image on the page. Here's where you need a special version of the `<IMG>` tag, which includes yet another attribute: `<USEMAP>`. If you name your map *example*, and the image file used is *example.gif*, then the tag looks like this:

```
<img src="example.gif" usemap="#example">
```

So, the entire piece of coding could look something like:

```
<img src="example.gif" width="500" height="500" border="0" usemap="#example">
<map name="example">
<area shape="rect" coords="75,134,152,204" href="example1.htm" >
<area shape="rect" coords="165,81,251,158" href="example2.htm" >
<area shape="rect" coords="51,43,126,107" href="example3.htm" >
</map>
```

Notice how the reference for the usemap has a hash (#) sign in front of it. Usemap has a standard URL as its value. Since we are referring to a map-name on the same page, we precede it with a hash. We could, if we had wanted, store the mapping information on a separate page and reference this with a standard URL.

Lists

Numbered lists
Bulleted lists
Glossary lists
Nesting lists

When using a word processor such as MS Word, it's very common to use bulleted lists. On the formatting toolbar there are even a couple of icons that allow you to make numbered lists and lists with various bullet symbols.

HTML also allows you to create lists, and it recognises three different types:

- **Numbered**
- **Bulleted**
- **Glossary.**

All lists have opening and closing tags, and each list item also has a tag.

Numbered lists

Numbered lists are also known as **Ordered** lists and make themselves known to HTML with `<OL>`...`</OL>` tags. In addition, each item within the list begins with a `<LI>` tag (although you don't have to specify the closing tag `</LI>`).

You would normally use numbered lists when you want to specify an order for certain items – such as giving instructions to a 'new' man for ironing a shirt.

1. Take shirt from washing line
2. Switch on iron
3. Put up ironing board
4. Fumble around
5. Look pathetic
6. Ask wife to show you once again how it should be done.

Let's see how to code that in HTML…

```
<ol>
  <li>Take shirt from washing line
  <li>Switch on iron
  <li>Put up ironing board
  <li>Fumble around
  <li>Look pathetic
  <li>Ask wife to show you once again how it should be done.
</ol>
```

There is no necessity to start a new line for each `<LI>` tag, although doing so makes it easier to see what is going on when you come to look for errors at a later date. But you could have written the entire lot of code as:

```
<ol><li>Take shirt from washing line<li>Switch on iron<li>Put up ironing board<li>Fumble around<li>Look pathetic<li>Ask wife to show you once again how it should be done.</ol>
```

Each of the `<LI>` tags tells the browser to force a new line and number in sequence the words that follow. We can see how this looks when we load the file into Netscape (Figure 6.1).

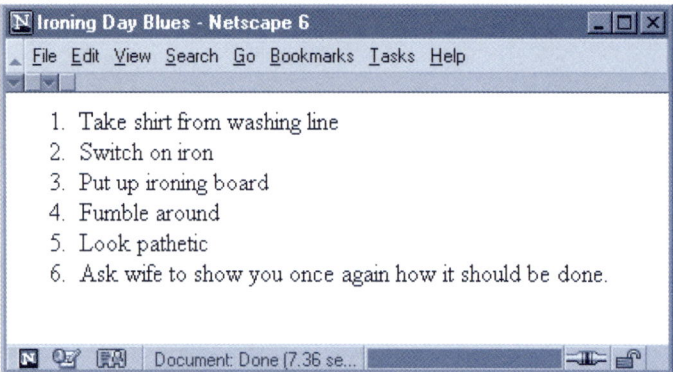

Figure 6.1 An ordered (numbered) list.

Just as Word allows you to format the way your numbering looks, so too does HTML give you a range of attributes to add to your `<OL>` tags. They are:

1   Arabic numerals are used – 1, 2, 3, 4, 5, etc.
I   Roman numerals are used – I, II, III, IV, V, etc.
i   Lower case Roman numerals are used – i, ii, iii, iv, v, etc.
A   Upper case letters are used – A, B, C, D, E, etc.
a   Lower case letters are used – a, b, c, d, e, etc.

So, entering an 'a' into the `<OL>` tag to create:

```
<ol type="a">
```

would appear as Figure 6.2 in Netscape.

6: Lists

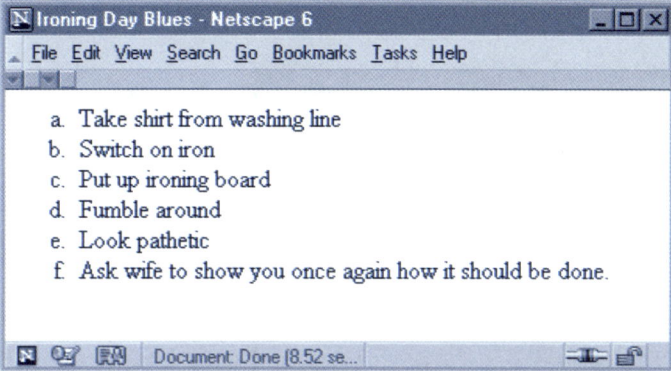

Figure 6.2 An ordered list with the 'type="a"' attribute.

You can even change the type of numbering halfway through a list (although we can't think why you would want to) by adding the type attribute to an `<LI>` tag. So:

```
<ol type="a">
   <li>Take shirt from washing line
   <li>Switch on iron
   <li type="A">Put up ironing board
   <li>Fumble around
   <li>Look pathetic
   <li>Ask wife to show you once again how it should be done.
</ol>
```

would create a list as shown in Figure 6.3.

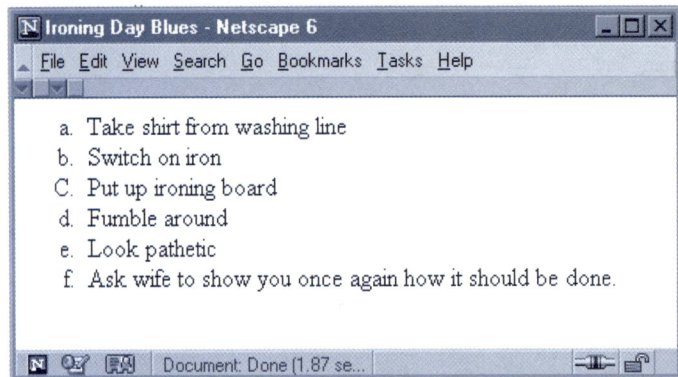

Figure 6.3 Adding an attribute to one of the `<LI>` tags.

You can also determine from what number or letter you want your counting to start. For instance, if we added the tag `<OL TYPE="1" START="3">`, you could expect your numbered list to start with the number 3.

And again, if you want to break the sequence of numbering, there is nothing to stop you adding the **VALUE** attribute to an `<LI>` tag in the middle of a list:

```
<ol type="1" start="3">
  <li>Take shirt from washing line
  <li>Switch on iron
  <li value="7">Put up ironing board
```

```
    <li>Fumble around
    <li>Look pathetic
     <li>Ask wife to show you once again how it should be
done.
</ol>
```

would appear as shown in Figure 6.4.

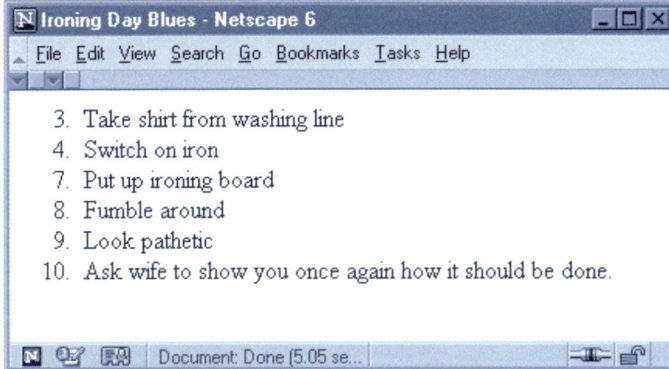

Figure 6.4 Switching numbers in an ordered list.

Bulleted lists

Bulleted lists are also known as unordered lists, since the bullet points inserted against each individual list entry do not normally denote any special order in the listing.

You create bulleted lists in exactly the same way as numbered lists, except that instead of using <OL>...</OL> tags, you use <UL>...</UL> tags.

Hence, if we wanted to create a list of drinks for the Website of a cocktail bar, we could enter:

```
<ul>
    <li>Sloe Screw
    <li>Jungle Juice
    <li>Black Russian
    <li>Tom Collins
    <li>Pink Gin
</ul>
```

and we would expect to see something like Figure 6.5.

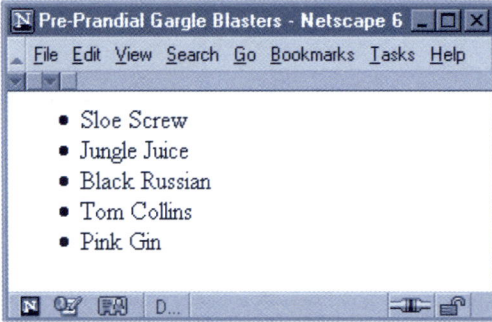

Figure 6.5 A bulleted list.

We can assign various attributes to an unordered list, in order to change the shape of the bullet:

- The default style is **Disc** which is a filled-in circle
- **Square** is, as you might have guessed, a square
- **Circle** shows an unfilled circle.

And if we enter the code below, we should be able to see something akin to Figure 6.6.

```
<ul type="disc">
   <li>Sloe Screw </li>
   <li>Jungle Juice </li>
   <li>Black Russian </li>
   <li>Tom Collins </li>
   <li>Pink Gin </li>
</ul>
<ul type="circle">
   <li>Sloe Screw </li>
   <li>Jungle Juice </li>
   <li>Black Russian </li>
   <li>Tom Collins </li>
   <li>Pink Gin </li>
</ul>
<ul type="square">
```

```
    <li>Sloe Screw </li>
    <li>Jungle Juice </li>
    <li>Black Russian </li>
    <li>Tom Collins </li>
    <li>Pink Gin </li>
</ul>
```

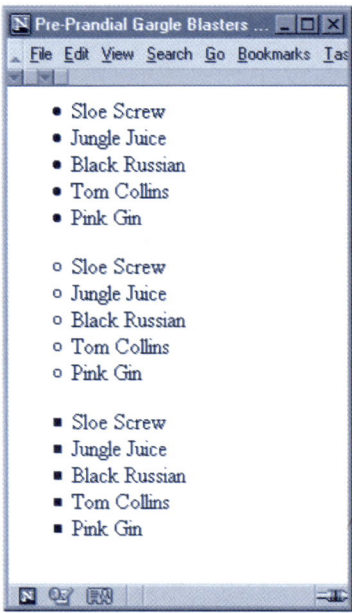

Figure 6.6 Three types of bullet can be used in your HTML coding.

Glossary lists

A Glossary list is different from the types of list we have considered so far. It has two parts to it – a header, or 'term', followed by a definition.

The Glossary list is enclosed in `<DL>`...`</DL>` tags with the header using `<DT>` and the definition using `<DD>`.

Here's an example of how a glossary list might be created and what it would look like in Netscape (Figure 6.7).

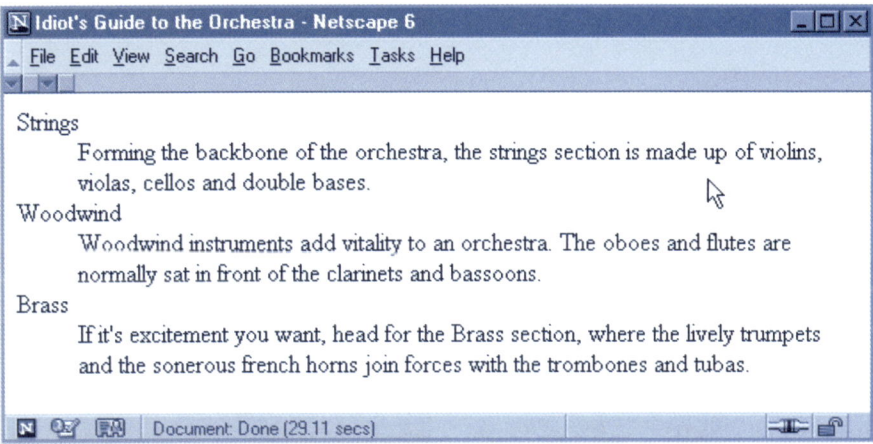

Figure 6.7 A glossary list invariably leaves terms and definitions on separate lines, and indents the definitions.

```
<DL>

<DT>Strings<DD>Forming the backbone of the orchestra, the
strings section is made up of violins, violas, cellos and
double bases.

<DT>Woodwind<DD>Woodwind instruments add vitality to an
orchestra. The oboes and flutes are normally sat in front
of the clarinets and bassoons.

<DT>Brass<DD>If it's excitement you want, head for the
Brass section, where the lively trumpets and the sonorous
French horns join forces with the trombones and tubas.

</DL>
```

Nesting lists

HTML is perfectly happy if you want to nest one list inside another one. For instance, you could have a numbered list with bullet point subdivisions. To make it easier to read, we've staggered the lines to group relevant bullets together:

```
<OL type="A">
  <LI>France
    <UL type="disc">
    <LI>Paris is the capital
    <LI>The French eat snails
    </UL>
  <LI>Germany
    <UL type="square">
```

```
      <LI>Moved their capital to Berlin
      <LI>The Germans love Sauerkraut
      </UL>
    <LI>Switzerland
      <UL type="circle">
      <LI>Berne is the federal capital
      <LI>The Swiss make wonderful chocolate
      </UL>
  </OL>
```

And the end result should look something like Figure 6.8.

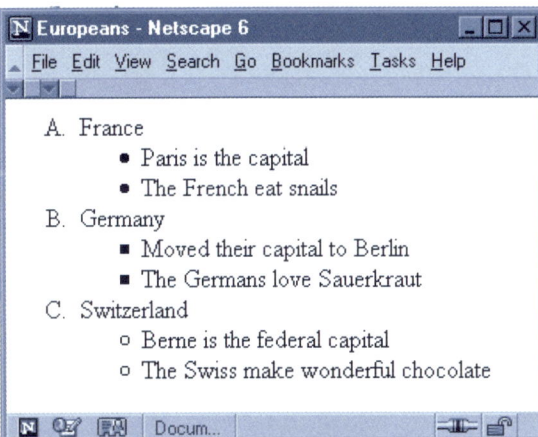

Figure 6.8 You can mix one type of list with another.

Tables 7

Table basics
Heading cells
Sizing and padding tables
Borders
Text layout in tables
Setting colours and backgrounds
Alignment
Spanning multiple rows and columns
Headers and footers
Frame and rule attributes

It was when tables were first introduced into HTML in the spring of 1995 that Web design went through a major shake-up. Not only could Web designers present their data in tabular format, but they could also use tables to give better control over page layout and positioning.

We wouldn't dream of suggesting that you hand-code all your tables, since it is only something that masochists should consider. However, even if you create tables using an HTML editor, you still need to understand how they work.

Table basics

For this chapter, we're going to call on Microsoft's FrontPage to help us with the coding and we'll begin by creating a table three cells wide by three cells tall (Figure 7.1).

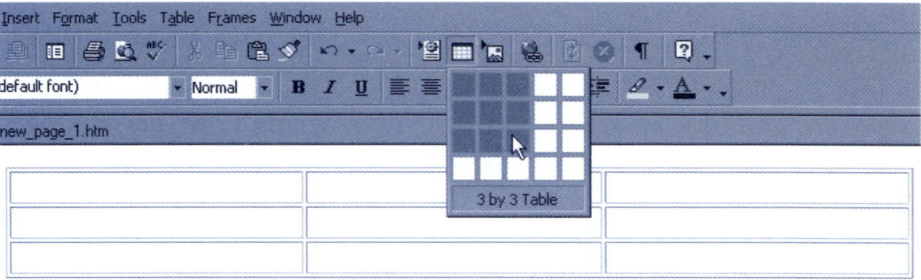

Figure 7.1 Start by creating a 3 × 3 table.

Depending on which HTML editor you use, you will either get the coding below, or something very similar. Let's see what we've got!

```
<table border="1" width="100%">
  <tr>
    <td width="33%"> </td>
    <td width="33%"> </td>
    <td width="34%"> </td>
  </tr>
  <tr>
    <td width="33%"> </td>
    <td width="33%"> </td>
    <td width="34%"> </td>
  </tr>
  <tr>
    <td width="33%"> </td>
    <td width="33%"> </td>
    <td width="34%"> </td>
  </tr>
</table>
```

The first thing you'll notice is that the entire table is enclosed within `<TABLE>`...`</TABLE>` tags. But there are also some other tags there that play very important parts.

If you compare the code with Figure 7.1, you should be able to see that each row begins and ends with `<TR>`...`</TR>` tags. Each of these rows is filled with cells – enclosed in `<TD>`...`</TD>` tags. These latter tags are known as data tags. The cells that they define can contain text, images, videos, animations ... in fact, just about anything.

We'll look at the border and width attributes in a moment. For the moment, though, what are those ` ` entries doing there?

FrontPage has put them there for a reason, yet it's difficult initially to see what they do. So let's experiment and remove some of them. Are you game? OK. Let's remove every second instance so that we end up with:

```
<table border="1" width="100%">
  <tr>
    <td width="33%"></td>
    <td width="33%"> </td>
    <td width="34%"></td>
  </tr>
  <tr>
    <td width="33%"> </td>
    <td width="33%"></td>
    <td width="34%"> </td>
  </tr>
  <tr>
    <td width="33%"></td>
    <td width="33%"> </td>
```

```
      <td width="34%"></td>
   </tr>
</table>
```

Now save the file and open it up in your favourite browser (Figure 7.2).

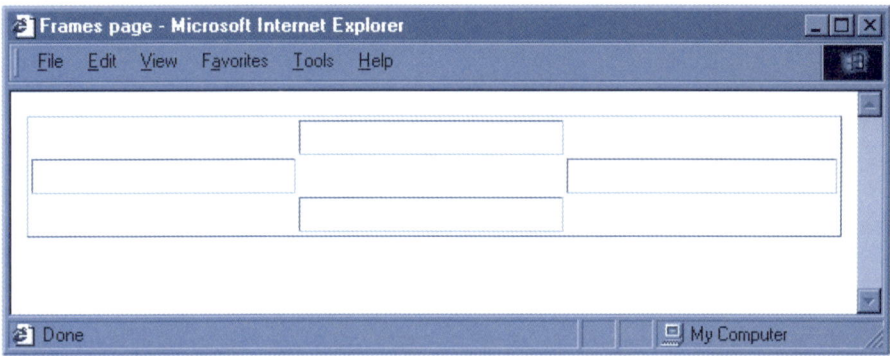

Figure 7.2 What's happened to those cells?

The secret lies in the fact that ` ` is a special character that stands in for a space. The fact is that HTML wants to see something inside a table cell, but it's not all that choosy what it sees. Instead of the ` ` we could have inserted a `<BR>` line break or any character whatsoever. Without anything, the cell simply disappears in a puff of blue smoke.

Let's add some text into the various cells. We'll make some of it bold, some italic, and some a combination of the two.

```
                <table border="1" width="100%">
                  <tr>
                    <td width="33%"><b>a</b></td>
                    <td width="33%"><b>b</b></td>
                    <td width="34%"><b>c</b></td>
                  </tr>
                  <tr>
                    <td width="33%"><i>d</i></td>
                    <td width="33%"><i>e</i></td>
                    <td width="34%"><i>f</i></td>
                  </tr>
                  <tr>
                    <td width="33%"><b><i>g</i></b></td>
                    <td width="33%"><b><i>h</i></b></td>
                    <td width="34%"><b><i>j</i></b></td>
                  </tr>
                </table>
```

If you've been keeping up so far you should end up with something similar to that shown in Figure 7.3.

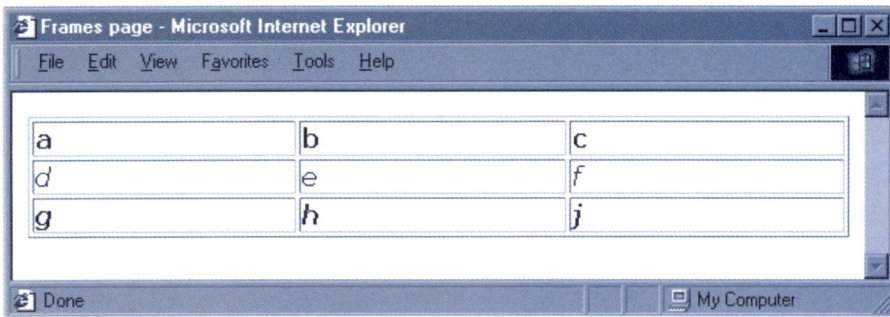

Figure 7.3 Text can have any number of formatting options applied to it.

Heading cells

There is a variation on the `<TD>` tag which is useful if you want to create a heading in one or more cells. Try using `<TH>`...`</TH>` to see what it does to the contents of a cell (Figure 7.4).

You can also add a caption at the top of your table by using (what else!) the `<CAPTION>`...`</CAPTION>` tags. These can be emboldened, italicised, coloured or anything else you might care to do. Let's make it bold...

```
<table border="1" width="100%">
  <Caption><b>This is a table <b></Caption>
  <tr>
    <th width="33%">header1</th>
    <th width="33%">header2</th>
    <th width="34%">header3</th>
```

```
      </tr>
      <tr>
        <td width="33%">d</td>
        <td width="33%">e</td>
        <td width="34%">f</td>
      </tr>
      <tr>
        <td width="33%">g</td>
        <td width="33%">h</td>
        <td width="34%">j</td>
      </tr>
    </table>
```

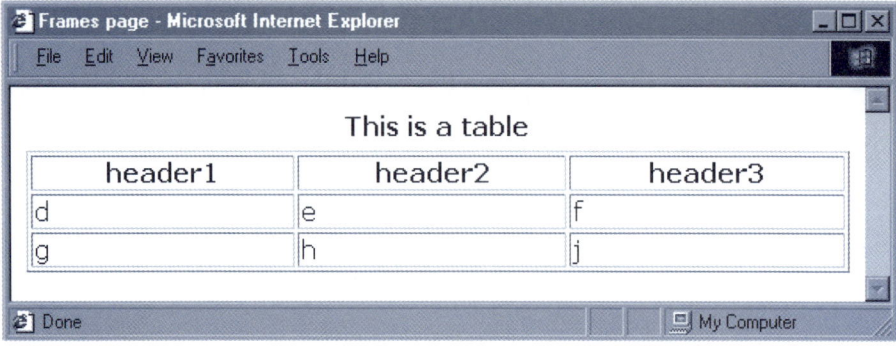

Figure 7.4 The <TH> tag converts a cell into a heading cell whilst <Caption> adds an overall header.

Sizing and padding tables

We've already seen that tables can have a **WIDTH** attribute assigned to them, as can the individual cells. FrontPage decided to set these automatically in percentages, but you can also set widths in absolute values by stating the number of pixels they should take up.

To make the table fit the total width of the screen, however big that might be, use the `<TABLE WIDTH="100%">` attribute. If you want it to fill half the screen width, set the attribute to `<TABLE WIDTH="50%">` and so on.

The problem with using absolute values for setting your table widths is that when the browser window is reduced to less than the size of the table, it forces the window to scroll across or down the page to accommodate the table.

You can determine the amount of space between the edges of a cell and its contents. By default, HTML interprets a default spacing of one pixel, but you can increase this to whatever you want. Simply add the **CELLPADDING** attribute to your `<TABLE>` tag and follow it with the number of pixels you require (Figure 7.5).

```
<table border="1" >
<tr>
<td >
<p align="center">here is a table with cell padding set at 1 pixel</p>
</td>
</tr>
```

If you try to make the table too narrow for the data that it is attempting to hold, then your browser will get confused. It will do its best to get as close to your desired sizes as possible, but expect some weird effects.

```
</table>
<p>
<table border="1" cell padding="10" >
<tr>
<td >here is a table with cell padding set at 10 pixels</td>
</tr>
</table>
```

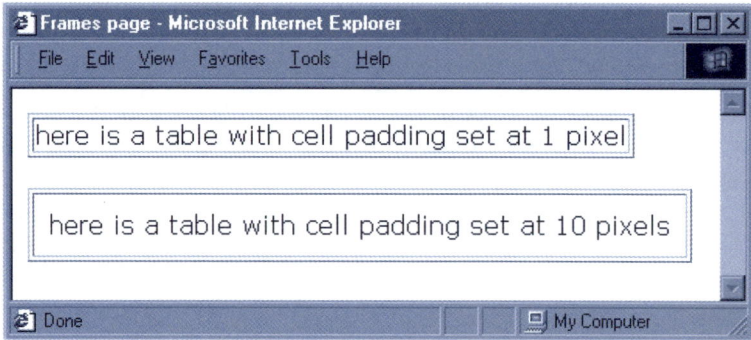

Figure 7.5 Use cell padding to alter the spacing around your text.

Similar to cell padding is another attribute called **CELLSPACING** which sets the amount of space between cells. By default, cell spacing is set at 2.

Experiment by changing the values attributed to the cell spacing in the `<TABLE>` tag as below (Figure 7.6):

    <TABLE CELLSPACING="10">

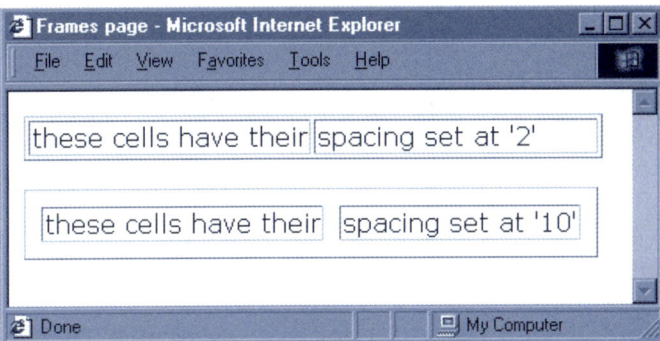

Figure 7.6 Cell spacing sets the space between cells.

Borders

We saw earlier on that FrontPage inserts a default border width of one pixel, but you can set it to any value you like (Figure 7.7). If you set the value to zero, the border becomes invisible – something which becomes extremely useful when you want to place items on a page, but don't want the table to become visible.

Text layout in tables

When you fill a cell with text, you can force new line breaks by the judicious insertion of `<BR>` and `<P>` tags. But what happens if the browser tries to force

HTML

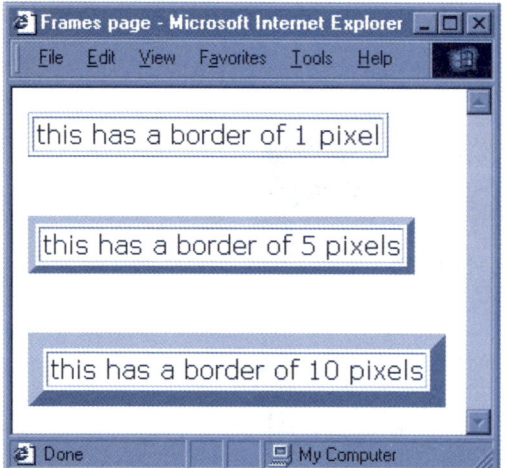

Figure 7.7 You can set the border value to any number of pixels you choose.

Be careful setting NOWRAP and line breaks by hand since you can never know what screen widths your viewers will be using when they see the results of your efforts. You could inadvertently end up in a worse mess than you started with!

a new line break when you don't want it to? The answer lies in an attribute called **NOWRAP** which you enter into the `<TD>` or `<TH>` tags. You can always add `<BR>` elements where you want them and force the browser to display the contents of the cell the way you want.

Setting colours and backgrounds

Just as you can set the background colour or image of a Web page, so too can you set the background colour or image of a table or even of an individual cell. In the same way we used the **BGCOLOR** attribute in the `<BODY>` tag (see page 51) the value of BGCOLOR in the `<TABLE>` or `<TD>` tags is specified in hexadecimal or as a named colour (see the Appendix).

In terms of priority, a table background overrides that of the page background. A row background takes priority over that of the table, whilst a cell's background takes absolute priority over anything else. Consider the following and then compare it with Figure 7.8.

```
<body bgcolor="#00FFFF">
<table border="1" width="50%" bgcolor="#ffff99">
 <tr>
<td width="33%" bgcolor="#000000"><p> </p>
</td>
<td width="33%"><p> </p>
</td>
<td width="34%" bgcolor="#000000"><p> </p>
</td>
</tr>
<tr>
<td width="33%"><p> </p>
</td>
<td width="33%" bgcolor="#000000"><p> </p></td>
<td width="34%"><p> </p>
</td>
</tr>
```

HTML

```
<tr>
<td width="33%" bgcolor="#000000"><p> </p>
</td>
<td width="33%"><p> </p>
</td>
<td width="34%" bgcolor="#000000"><p> </p>
</td>
</tr>
</table>
</body>
```

Figure 7.8 Priority orders of cell/page backgrounds.

You can also change the colours of the border by using **BORDERCOLOR** as yet another attribute to go in the `<TABLE>` tag.

Alignment

Another way you can alter the appearance of your tables is to set the alignment attributes – whether you want your cell contents centred, left or right aligned, for instance. You use the **ALIGN** attribute to set the horizontal alignment, whilst **VALIGN** sets the alignment vertically – Top, Bottom or Middle.

We saw how to align images in Chapter 3, so we don't need to repeat it here since the alignment attributes are set in exactly the same way.

Spanning multiple rows and columns

Creating tables with single entries in each cell is fairly straightforward, once you have mentally been able to compartmentalise each separate pair of `<TD>` and `<TR>` tags. The fun begins when you want to 'cross the divide' between two or more rows or columns in order to create special (and not so special) effects.

We're going to call on the help of our old friend FrontPage again to create a table with a cell that spans across two columns (see Figure 7.9). Create a table two columns wide by three rows deep, add some text into each cell, highlight the top two cells and then right-click within this highlighted environment and choose *Merge* from the sub-menu that appears. (Almost all Web editors offer this facility of merging cells, but, of course, they all have their own unique way of doing it. You will just have to experiment with your own editor to see how it creates merged cells.)

HTML

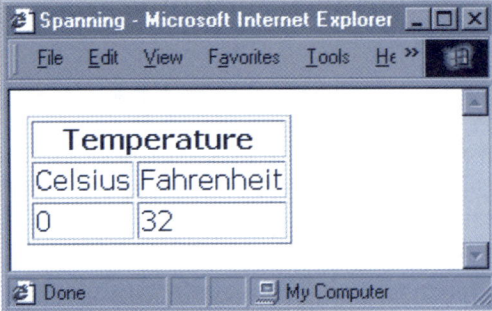

Figure 7.9 Spanning across two columns.

Let's take a look at what code is produced.

```
<table border="1">
  <tr>
    <th colspan="2">Temperature</th>
  </tr>
  <tr>
    <td>Celsius</td>
    <td>Fahrenheit</td>
  </tr>
  <tr>
    <td>0</td>
```

```
    <td>32</td>
  </tr>
</table>
```

The header row has effectively been merged into one cell, by using the **COLSPAN** attribute (in this case, to two columns' width). We could have merged two cells vertically if we had wanted, and for this we would have seen the **ROWSPAN** attribute being used.

Cells always span downward and to the right. So if you want a cell that spans several columns, you have to add your COLSPAN instruction in the cell furthest to the left. To span across different rows, make sure the ROWSPAN attribute is placed in the topmost cell.

Let's get more adventurous and make a couple of spannings – one across two columns and another across two rows (Figure 7.10).

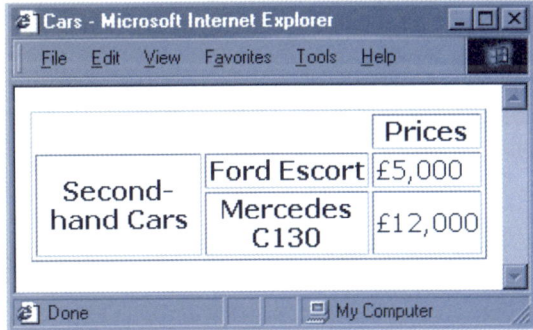

Figure 7.10 Spanning across rows and columns.

```html
<table border="1">
  <tr>
    <td colspan="2"></td>
    <th>Prices</th>
  </tr>
  <tr>
    <th rowspan="2">Second-hand Cars</th>
    <th>Ford Escort</th>
    <td>£5,000</td>
  </tr>
  <tr>
    <th>Mercedes C130</th>
    <td>£12,000</td>
  </tr>
</table>
```

Here you can see the use of both COLSPAN and ROWSPAN. The top left cell spans two columns, hence the use of:

```html
<td colspan="2">.
```

The bottom left cell spans two rows, hence the use of:

```html
<th rowspan="2">
```

You'll see that we haven't entered a special character space into the top left cell, so we aren't surprised to see that its cell border is missing. Also, you will have noticed that, because we have entered header information into various cells, some cells are defined with <TD> whilst others have <TH>.

Headers and footers

One of the greatest frustrations when printing out someone else's tabular data from a Website is when a table spans across two or more pieces of paper. How do you remember which column is which? Wouldn't it be just great if you could have a header row and a footer row that appeared in every grouping printed out from that table?

Well, judging from the number of Websites using tables, you might well have believed that this is something we'll have to keep on dreaming about for some time. But those awfully clever people in charge of HTML solved the problem a long time ago by introducing three new table tags:

- <THEAD>
- <TBODY>
- <TFOOT>

The head element contains information about the columns in the main part of the table. It is placed immediately after the <TABLE> tag and begins with the <THEAD> tag (but you don't actually need to use a </THEAD> closing tag).

Perhaps surprisingly, you next have to define the <TFOOT> section *before* the main body of the table. This is because the browser might have to have this information if the main body information is spread across two pages. Once again, you can forget about `</TFOOT>` if you want to.

Next comes the `<TBODY>` section – or, to put it better, next comes the `<TBODY>` section or sections. You can have as many `<TBODY>` sections as you like (we'll see why this is useful in a moment). Finally, you close in the normal way with a `</TABLE>` tag.

As usual, a little bit of sample code should make things much clearer. Although the whole point of a header and footer is when you have enormously long tables, we'll make things easy by having a table just three cells wide by three cells deep.

```
<table border="1">

  <thead>
  <tr>
  <th> Race</th>
  <th> Time</th>
  <th> Winner</th>
  </tr>
  </thead>

  <tfoot>
  <tr>
  <th> Race</th>
  <th> Time</th>
```

```
      <th> Winner</th>
   </tr>
</tfoot>

<tbody> <tr>
      <td>No 1</td>
      <td>13:20</td>
      <td>White Rabbit</td>
   </tr>
   <tr>
      <td>No 2</td>
      <td>13:50</td>
      <td>The Parrot</td>
   </tr>
   <tr>
      <td>No 3</td>
      <td>14:20</td>
      <td>Bumper</td>
   </tr>
   </tbody>

</table>
```

Take a look at Figure 7.11 to see how Internet Explorer interprets the above. Remember that you must have the same number of columns in your <THEAD> section as in the other sections as you will otherwise come up with some very unexpected results.

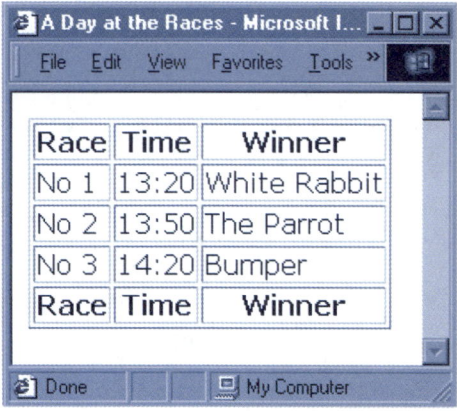

Figure 7.11 Using headers and footers in a table.

Frame and rule attributes

Another set of attributes that appears to have escaped the notice of many Web developers allows you to determine which sides of your tables and cells are visible or are made invisible.

Both the **FRAME** and **RULES** attributes are added to the `<TABLE>` element. The former affects the way the external border of a table is rendered, whilst the latter affects the rules in between the various cells.

Let's start with the **FRAME** attributes:

ABOVE	Renders only the top side of the border.
BELOW	Renders only the bottom border.
BORDER	All four sides of the border are shown.
BOX	Exactly the same as BORDER.
HSIDES	The top and bottom sides are shown.
LHS	Renders the left hand side of the border.
RHS	Renders the right hand side of the border.
VOID	No sides of the external border are visible.
VSIDES	The left and right hand sides are shown.

The default value is VOID if you do not specify any attribute.

And now for the **RULES** attributes:

ALL	Rules will appear between all rows and columns.
COLS	Rules will be inserted between columns only.
GROUPS	Rules appear between groups as defined by `<THEAD>`, `<TFOOT>` and `<TBODY>`.

NONE   No rules are drawn around any cells.

ROWS   Rules are drawn only between rows.

The default value is NONE. Pay particular attention to the GROUPS attribute. Do you remember that we said you could have more than one `<TBODY>` section in a table? Now you know why!

So let's change the first line of the coding above to read:

```
<table border="1" frame="hsides" rules="groups">
```

and see how this changes the layout of our table in Figure 7.12.

Figure 7.12 Our table now has a complete change of style thanks to the RULES and FRAME attributes.

Style sheets

8

How style sheets work
External style sheets
Creating a style sheet
Embedded style sheets
Cascading?
Margins and padding
Backgrounds
Borders
Text appearance
Text alignment
Inline styles

Throughout this book we have been looking at different ways to format text and images – defining the appearance of a headline by specifying its font, colour or size, for example. Since the appearance, though, of Netscape and Explorer versions 4 and above, a much more useful and browser-friendly weapon has been added to the Web designer's arsenal.

Cascading style sheets allow you to create a global specification of typefaces, font colours, background colours, graphics, margins, spacing, positioning ... and a whole lot more. In fact, with version two style sheets (CSS2), which are recognised by version 5 browsers, you can even design aural style sheets that speak elements of the Web page whilst also defining spatial audio and stereo settings!

How style sheets work

Style sheets combine the normal HTML rules of tags – such as `<H1>` – with properties such as `color:red`. A CSS style rule is made up of two parts:

- **Selector**: which is normally an HTML tag.
- **Declaration**: which defines the properties and values associated with them.

For example, you could define a header in the following way:

```
H1 {color: red}
```

or a paragraph style:

```
P {font-family: Arial, Helvetica, sans-serif; color: black}
```

8: Style sheets

There are three ways that you can apply style sheets to Web pages:

1. **External style sheets**
2. **Embedded style sheets**
3. **Inline styles.**

We'll look at each of these in turn.

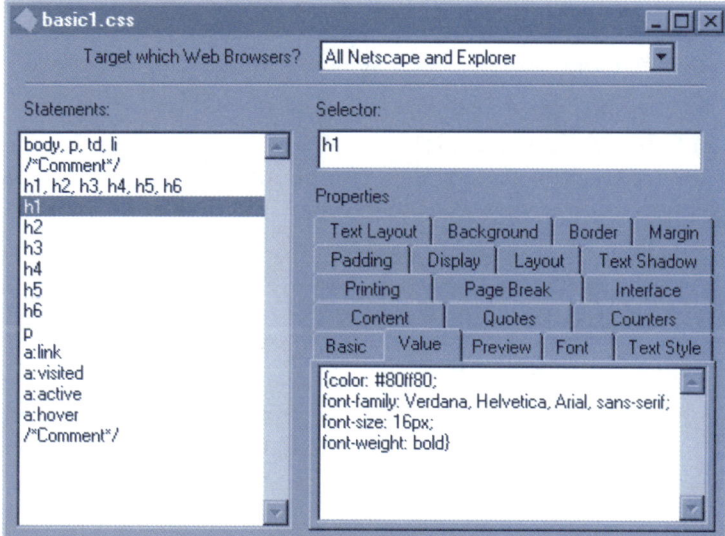

Figure 8.1 Defining styles using Style Master.

Once again, it's worth remembering that there are plenty of HTML editors such as Dreamweaver and FrontPage – as well as specific style sheet editors such as TopStyle and Style Master (Figure 8.1) – that make the creation of style sheets an absolute doddle!

External style sheets

When you're designing a Website, it is normal to have a consistent look and feel across all your pages. Rather than defining the look and feel of every element of every page, you can define a general set of styles to be applied right across the site. What a time saving, not to mention a substantial decrease in the size of your pages!

Another huge advantage of defining styles in this way is that if, say, you suddenly decided that your snazzy blue headlines would look much better in red, then with one quick change in the style sheet, you can change the look of every page in one fell swoop.

Style sheets, like HTML pages, are basically raw ASCII text with a special extension of their own. External style sheets can be identified by their **.css** extension. You link a particular style sheet using the `<LINK>` tag.

So, if you have a style sheet called *styles.css* (we'll see how to create one of these in a moment) and you want to link it to your HTML page, you would insert a link into your `<HEAD>` element like this:

```
<LINK REL="stylesheet" HREF="styles.css">
```

Note the use of the REL attribute. If you are feeling generous, you can allow your visitors to choose whether to use your style definitions or to use their own defaults.

REL is used to specify whether your style should be **persistent** – that is, your style is used whatever the user wants; **default** – where the user can disable it if she wants; or **alternate** – where the user is given a choice.

As the whole point of using style sheets is to let your visitors see the pages exactly as you intended, it's not necessarily a good idea to let your visitors override your design, but that's up to you!

If you define your style sheet link as shown above, it will create a persistent style. If you were to add a **TITLE** attribute such as `TITLE="mainstyle"` then your style sheet will be the default style. If, however, you change `REL="stylesheet"` to `REL="alternate stylesheet"`, you can offer your user choices of his own.

Creating a style sheet

We mentioned earlier that a style sheet is simply an ASCII text document with the .css extension applied to it. So let's define a very simple style sheet and attach it to a Web page.

Use Notepad (or some other plain text editor) and type in the following lines of code. (In the future you will probably want to use a styles editor – Figure 8.2 – but it's a useful exercise to go through the tedious bottom-up process now.)

```
Body {background-color: #ffff80; color: #ff0000; font-family: Verdana, Helvetica, Arial, sans-serif; font-weight: bold}
a:link {color: #0000ff}
a:visited {color: #00ff00}
a:active {color: #ff0000}
a:hover {color: #ffff00}
```

Save this and give it a name – such as *mystyles.css*.

HTML

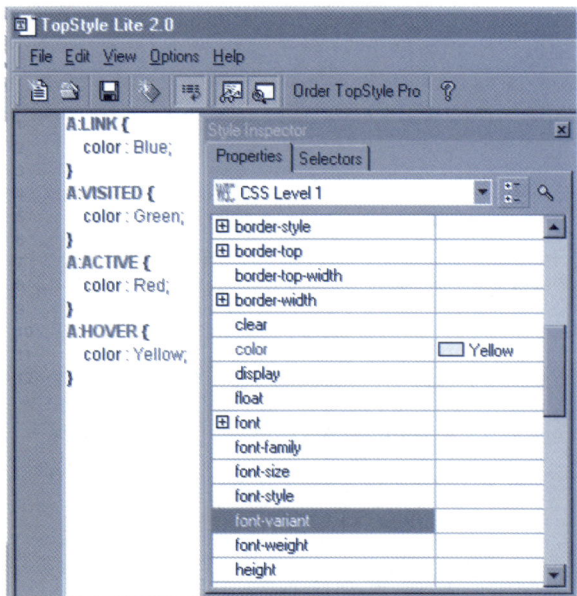

Figure 8.2 We could have used a styles editor to save time.

In the header section (between the <HEAD>...</HEAD> tags) of a Web page insert the following link:

```
<LINK REL="stylesheet" HREF="mystyles.css">
```

And that's it. You've just created your first style sheet and linked it to a Web page. Now, what does it do?

In the first section:

```
Body {background-color: #ffff80; color: #ff0000; font-family:
Verdana, Helvetica, Arial, sans-serif; font-weight: bold}
```

we're telling the browser that we want a light yellow background to the page (`#ffff80`) with a red typeface (`#ff0000`). That type should, by preference, be Verdana, or if the computer on which it being viewed does not have Verdana, then it should be displayed in Helvetica, or failing that, Arial or still failing that it should use whatever sans-serif font it can find. It should also display in bold text.

Next we have defined a number of link attributes that determine what happens to a hyperlink – whether it is sitting there minding its own business (`#0000ff`), or whether you hover over it with your mouse (`#ffff00`), whether it is active (`#ff0000`) or if you have already visited that linked page (`#00ff00`).

Embedded style sheets

Unlike external style sheets, embedded style sheets have style rules embedded within standard HTML pages. We've already commented that external style sheets are great for giving the same look and feel to an entire Website; so why should we bother with embedded sheets?

Well, you might, for example, want an opening home page to create a splash and then go into a more sedate site from there; or one page might need different colourings from the rest in order to make it stand out in some way. Whatever the reason, it wouldn't make sense to create an external style sheet just for one page. Instead we would use an embedded style sheet for that page only and an external style sheet for all the others.

Many people don't bother with having embedded style sheets, preferring instead to define separate styles within the external sheet and just label the one-off page with one-off styles within this external style sheet.

The one thing about style sheets, though, is that you can define your styles once, and then have everything else isolated from these style statements. So even in our embedded style sheets, we keep all the definitions together within the `<HEAD>` tags.

Embedded style sheets are defined by placing the following line within your `<HEAD>` section:

```
<STYLE TYPE="text/css">
```

You will need a closing `</STYLE>` tag at the end of your style definitions; but in the case of embedded style sheets it is normal to place your entire style rules within comment tags since if you don't, older browsers might try to display the rules as text.

So, using the example above, we could put the following code into our page header:

```
<STYLE TYPE="text/css">
<!–
Body {background-color: #ffff80; color: #ff0000; font-family: Verdana, Helvetica, Arial, sans-serif; font-weight: bold}
a:link {color: #0000ff}
a:visited {color: #00ff00}
a:active {color: #ff0000}
a:hover {color: #ffff00}
-->
</STYLE>
```

Cascading?

At the beginning of this chapter we used the term *cascading* style sheets. Indeed, we have seen the file extension is defined with *.css*. So what do we mean by this term?

Simply put, there is a critical order that is applied to styles when you have more than one type of style definition.

1. The styles in an external style sheet are applied first.
2. Embedded styles are then recognised and take precedence over the external styles.
3. Finally inline styles (which we'll be looking at shortly) override both external and embedded styles.

Margins and padding

We've seen that style sheets are a great way of defining how your text looks on a browser-viewed Web page. However, CSS allows you to define so much more, that we've only just scratched the surface up till now.

Take margins and padding, for example. We all know how easy it is to define these items in most word processors, but CSS allows you to define them for your Web pages too.

Some of the most commonly used page layout items are **margin** and **padding** – which you can set in numerical lengths, percentages, or auto.

The unit lengths are expressed in relative or absolute values thus:

- **em**   Size of the relevant font.
- **ex**   The x-height of the relevant font.
- **px**   Pixels relative to the device the page is being viewed on.
- **pt**   Points.
- **in**   Inches.
- **cm**   Centimetres.
- **mm**   Millimetres.
- **pc**   Picas.

But you can also use a percentage value instead of a length unit for which you would specify + or –, followed by a number, followed by a percentage (%) sign.

You can determine the settings for just one side of the margin or padding if you want (in which case you would use margin-top, margin-left, padding-right and so on). And you can also define different values for the different sides in just one statement.

For instance, `margin: 50px, 70px` would assign 50 pixels to the top and bottom margins and 70 pixels to the left and right. Alternatively, `margin: 20px, 30px, 40px, 50px` would apply 20, 30, 40 and 50 pixels to the top, right, bottom and left margins respectively (Figure 8.3).

8: Style sheets

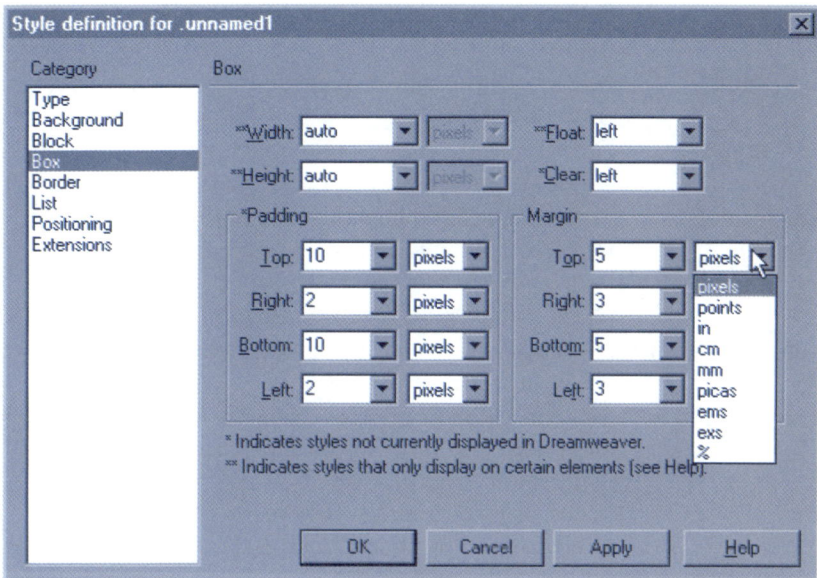

Figure 8.3 Defining margins and padding in Dreamweaver.

Backgrounds

We've already seen (Chapter 3) how to define background colours and images for a Web page. Using CSS, you can take much more control with no fewer than six properties for setting the background alone:

color	Sets the foreground element (usually text) using RGB colour values.
background-color	Sets a background colour using RGB, or specifying transparent.
background-image	Determines the background image with the URL of where the image has been stored.
background-repeat	Determines if and how the background image is repeated. Possible values are *repeat* (repeat horizontally and vertically), *repeat-x* (repeat horizontally), *repeat-y* (repeat vertically), *no-repeat*.
background-attachment	Determines if the background is fixed or scrolls with the document.
background-position	Sets the initial position of the background image using a keyword (*top*, *center*, *bottom*, *left*, *right*), by length – using x,y coordinates, where x and y are values in pixels, or by percentage (where 0% 0% is the upper left corner of the element and 100% 100% is the bottom right corner).
background	Sets one or more of the preceding properties in a single location.

So, to set the background image of an element we could use:

```
background-image: url(images/picture.gif); background-repeat: repeat
```

where *picture.gif*, which is stored in the *images* folder, is used to provide the background; and it is repeated both horizontally and vertically.

We could set our headline to be:

```
H1 {color: #FF0000;
padding-top: 10px; padding-bottom: 5px;
background-colour: #FFFF00}
```

which would give us a headline which had red text, a yellow background, and padding of 10 and 5 pixels top and bottom respectively.

Borders

In theory, CSS allows you to set border properties to any element in a page (Figure 8.4). Normally you would use these to set the borders in tables or around images.

border-style   You don't need to have a *solid* border. Instead you could try *none*, *dotted*, *dashed*, *double*, *groove*, *ridge*, *inset* and *outset*.

border-color   Colours can be set for each side of the border individually, or for all sides.

border-width   Set the width of each or every border to *thin*, *medium*, *thick* or specify a *length* value.

border   Use to set the *width*, *color* and/or *style* to all borders.

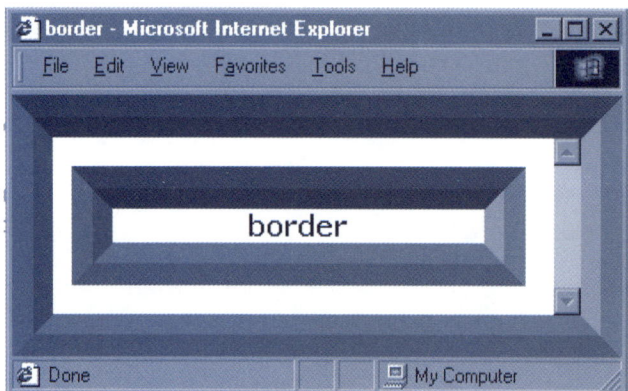

Figure 8.4 You can use CSS to set borders.

Text appearance

We've briefly seen how the appearance of your text can be changed using CSS, which offers you much more control than an ordinary <FONT> tag.

Here are the various CSS elements for text control:

font-family   You can specify one or more specific typefaces, or one of five generic font names – *serif*, *sans-serif*, *cursive*, *fantasy* or *monospace*. Be wary of using 'cursive' or 'fantasy' families since not all your visitors may have these font families installed.

font-size   Set the font size in absolute, relative or percentage terms.

font-style	*Oblique*, *italic* or *normal*. The first two often look the same.
font-weight	*Normal*, *bold*, *bolder* or *lighter*.
font-variant	*Small-caps* or *normal*.
font	Sets the font properties in one location.

Text alignment

By now, you won't be surprised to discover that CSS can give you the power to set the positioning of text on your Web pages. You can set very precise control of your positioning using some of the following elements (Figure 8.5). But be warned! Some of these controls are not recognised in certain versions of different browsers, so you really do need to try them out in each browser before you use them indiscriminately.

word-spacing	Used to add space between words. Use an absolute length or *normal*.
letter spacing	As above, but sets the spacing between letters.
line-height	Sets the distance between two lines, either as a multiple of the font size, or as an absolute value in pixels. You can also use percentage values, so *line-height: 2* is the same as *line-height: 200%*.
vertical-align	Sets the vertical alignment to *baseline*, *middle*, *sub*, *super*, *text-top* and *text-bottom* relative to the parent element.
text-align	Sets the alignment to *left*, *center*, *right* or *justify*.
text-decoration	*Underline*, *overline*, *line-through* or *blink*.

text-indent	Sets the indentation of the first line of formatted text, defined as an absolute value or a percentage of the element width.
white-space	*Normal* (as standard HTML), *pre* (just like `<PRE>`) and *nowrap* (you'll need to use ` ` to wrap a line).

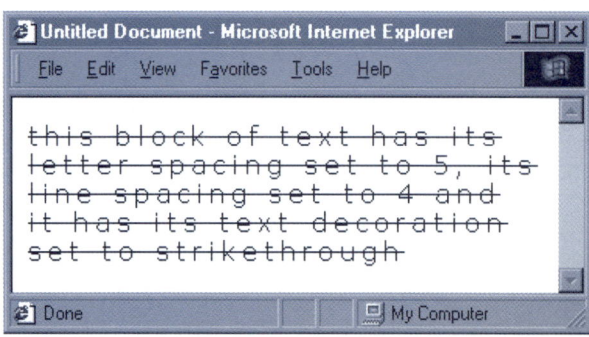

Figure 8.5 Text alignment in operation using CSS.

Inline styles

At last we can take a look at the third type of CSS. Inline styles allow you to apply style rules to an individual Web page element, rather than to an entire page. Inline styles are normally defined in either **Style** or **Class** attributes.

For instance, say you wanted to change one individual line to make it red and bold. You could, of course, use a pair of `<FONT>` tags. But a more elegant way is to use a style:

```
<P STYLE="color: red; font-weight: bold"> this line is red
and bold </P>
```

Then, of course, you might want more than one line changed to red and bold. Rather than define each line in this way, we can define a class and call it when entering the line in question. In the following example, let's define two paragraph styles – one using a sans-serif font, and another using a serif font.

We have to define the classes within the header:

```
<HTML>
<HEAD>
<STYLE TYPE="text/css">
<!–
P {font-family: sans-serif}
P.serif {font-family: serif}
-->
</STYLE>
</HEAD>
```

Note that we've defined 'normal' paragraphs in sans-serif and have defined a separate class called *P.serif*.

To apply the serif class to a specific paragraph we can enter some text within the `<BODY>` tags thus:

```
<P>This is sans-serif text </P>
<P CLASS="serif"> and this is serif text</P>
```

A further property – `<SPAN>` – can be used to apply styles to a portion of text, which is not contained within a specific HTML tag. For instance, you might want to apply a style to a couple of words contained within a sentence.

We might decide we want to define a class of font, which is cursive, green and 16pt. We can define the class within the `<HEAD>` section thus:

```
.CURSIVE {font-family: "cursive";
font-size: 16pt;
color: #00FF00}
```

which we can then apply to some text within the `<BODY>` section:

```
<P> Here's some <SPAN CLASS="cursive"> cursive </SPAN> text</P>
```

We've only been able to scratch the surface of what is available within cascading style sheets. Although not strictly HTML in their own right, it would be impossible not to include them within a book on this subject. Anyone who wants to get to grips with HTML cannot afford to ignore the many advantages that CSS brings.

Frames 9

What are frames?

Target

<BASE>

Framesets

<FRAME>

<NOFRAMES>

Frame borders

What are frames?

Have you ever wondered why it is that on some Websites the entire page changes whenever you click on a hyperlink, whereas with others, only parts of the Web page appear to change whilst others remain static and always visible?

The idea behind **frames** is that one master Web page can contain a number of smaller Web pages within it (each a full-scale HTML page in its own right) and clicking on a link in one of these pages can change the contents of another.

Most modern Web editors have the provision for creating framed Web pages. If ever you needed to understand the HTML behind a Web page, then when you use frames you will definitely be glad you learned some of HTML's basic principles. It doesn't matter how good you think FrontPage, Dreamweaver, or whatever, are, we can almost guarantee that you will need to tweak the settings once you have created frames in your favourite editor.

In this chapter we'll use MS FrontPage to demonstrate many of the features we are talking about, but the rules remain true for all of them. So let's start by creating a new frames page. We'll create one containing a banner frame along the top and a contents frame down the left-hand side of the page (Figure 9.1).

The 'banner' frame can contain messages and advertisements that you want displayed all the time when your visitors browse through your Website. The 'contents' frame will contain the navigation buttons, which will change the content within the 'main' frame. Remember, though, that although we have created three frames, each frame is a stand-alone HTML page in its own right (Figure 9.2).

9: Frames 139

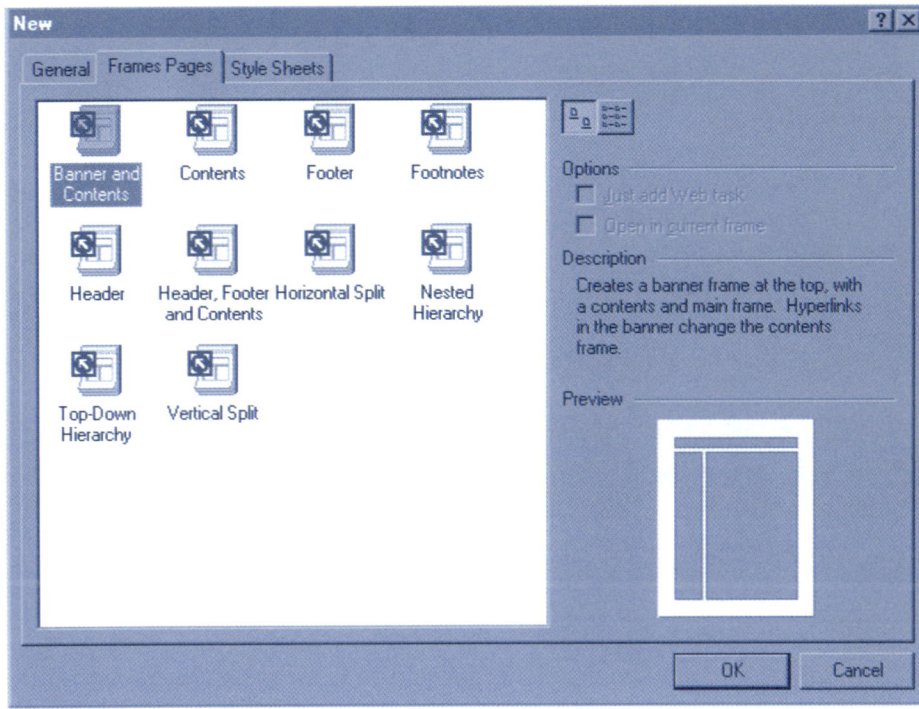

Figure 9.1 Creating a frames page in MS FrontPage.

HTML

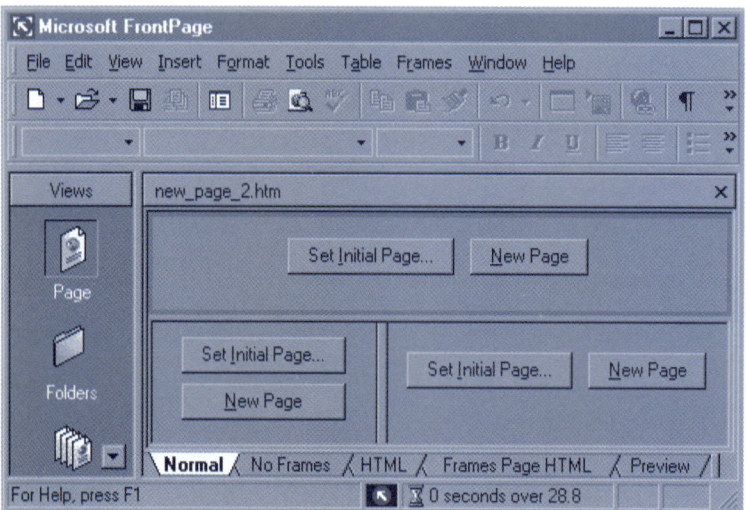

Figure 9.2 Each framed page is an HTML page in its own right.

Target

So let's take a look at some of the code set up for us by the Web page editor. Apart from the normal stuff at the top in the <HEAD> section, there is a **frameset** of instructions telling the browser how to display the different pages that make up the frame set.

```
<frameset rows="64,*">
  <frame name="banner" scrolling="no" noresize target="contents">
  <frameset cols="150,*">
    <frame name="contents" target="main">
    <frame name="main">
  </frameset>
```

Take a close look at this code. Do you see that each frame is given a name – in this case:

- **Banner**
- **Contents**
- **Main.**

There's also a new attribute that we have not come across before: **TARGET**.

The code is telling the browser that if there are any hyperlinks contained in the frame called *banner*, that they will change the contents of the frame marked *contents*. Similarly, any hyperlinks contained in the frame *contents* will change what is displayed in the frame called *main*.

TARGET is basically an attribute of the `<A>` tag. You could decide that you wanted on one particular occasion a hyperlink to change the contents of a different frame rather than its default frame. In this case you would code it thus:

```
TARGET="window_name"
```

HTML

If you attempt to get your hyperlink to load into a frame which doesn't exist, a new Web page will be opened to display the new page instead.

You can call the new window anything you like, except for the following target names, which have special meanings:

_blank   Creates a new window into which the hyperlinked page is displayed.

_self   Overlays the current frame with the hyperlinked page.

_parent   Forces the hyperlinked page to overlay the parent of the current document.

_top   Forces the linked page to overwrite the entire frameset.

To show this in practice, we'll take the framed page that we set up earlier and give names to each framed page before saving them (let's save then as *red.htm*, *green.htm* and *blue.htm*). Now change the background colours of these pages to red, green and blue respectively.

In the blue page (i.e. the *main* frame) add in two hyperlinks with the following code:

```
<a href="green.htm" target="banner"> Open Green page at top
</a>
<a href="red.htm" target="contents"> Open Red page at left
</a>
```

Now, if you view your page in a browser it should look something like Figure 9.3.

9: Frames

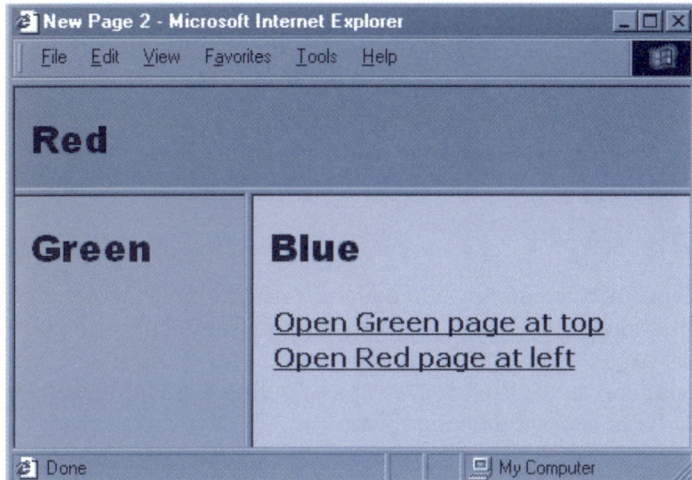

Figure 9.3 Our three-framed page with background colours and two links added.

Try clicking on the two links and see how they change the colours in the top and left-hand frames.

Next, try changing the code to the following:

```
<a href="green.htm" target="_blank"> Open Green page in new window</a>
<a href="red.htm" target="_self"> Open Red page in this window </a>
```

and then click on the two links. A new window should open up and load the green page, whilst the bottom link will have the effect of changing the blue frame to a red frame.

You can see, now, why frames give you the wherewithal to create a very neat navigational site whereby any buttons in a contents frame can change the makeup of the main page.

<BASE>

It's very common – especially when you have a contents frame in which you display your navigational buttons – for all the links in one framed page to point to targets in another frame. Instead of targeting each <A> link, it's often easier in such circumstances to use the <BASE> tag to define a global target for all the links on a page. It takes the following form:

    <BASE TARGET="window_name">

You will need to house this line of code in your <HEAD>...</HEAD> tags, but remember that if you include a new TARGET within your <BODY> section for a particular hyperlink, this will override the BASE TARGET instruction.

Framesets

Let's return to the set of instructions that MS FrontPage set up for us when we created a set of frames. We'll give you the full HTML code so that we can examine it in more detail.

Be aware that, if you use frames, there is no reason why someone couldn't simply insert the name of one of the framed pages and call that up in their browser without the benefit of loading the navigational frame with it. You might even require the visitor to only be able to view your complete frameset – for instance, you might have an advertisement in the banner frame which you insist your visitors must see if they are to be able to access the rest of your site. It is possible to get round this problem by using

>>

```
<html>
<head>
<title>New Page 2</title>
<meta name="GENERATOR" content="Microsoft FrontPage 4.0">
<meta name="ProgId" content="FrontPage.Editor.Document">
</head>

<frameset rows="64,*">
  <frame name="banner" scrolling="no" noresize target="contents" src="red.htm">
  <frameset cols="150,*">
    <frame name="contents" target="main" src="green.htm">
    <frame name="main" src="blue.htm" target="_self">
  </frameset>

  <noframes>
  <body>
  <p>This page uses frames, but your browser doesn't support them.</p>
  </body>
  </noframes>

</frameset>
</html>
```

*(Continued)
Javascript (see Chapter 10), but those few people still using older browsers (i.e. prior to version 3) won't be able to see your frames at all.*

Ignore what's contained in the <HEAD> section right now. We're particularly interested in the next bit contained within the tags <FRAMESET>... </FRAMESET>.

The first line of code defines how the window is to be split into two rows – in this case, one of 64 pixels and the other which fills the rest of the available space (denoted by an '*').

This setting has devoted an *absolute* value of 64 pixels to the banner frame. If we had wanted to, we could have devoted a *relative* value such as 20% so that as the browser window changed in size (perhaps with different screen resolutions) the window would have still taken up the same amount of room proportionately.

After defining the split into rows, the name of the first frame is given, along with any attributes for that frame. An instruction is then given to split the next frame into two columns – in this case 150 pixels and '*' (ie whatever room is left for it).

So what we have now got is a horizontal split into two frames, with the lower of these two frames being split vertically to give an overall content of three frames.

Left on their own, we wouldn't have an awful lot to see in our browser, because what we haven't yet defined is the source of each frame. Remember that we said that each frame is an HTML page in its own right.

<FRAME>

Earlier on we created three pages – *red.htm*, *blue.htm* and *green.htm*. We need to associate each of our frames (*banner*, *contents* and *main*) with these pages, and for this we use the <FRAME> tag. If, say, we had divided up a frame into three rows, we could define these three subframes as:

If our frame uses buttons, or some other graphic, it may be more sensible to use absolute frame values, since that way you can ensure there is always enough room for the graphics, regardless of what else is found in the rest of the page.

```
<FRAMESET ROWS="*,*,*">
<FRAME SRC="red.htm">
<FRAME SRC="blue.htm">
<FRAME SRC="green.htm">
</FRAMESET>
```

In our original example above, however, we have defined the *main* frame to start with *blue.htm*, the *contents* frame to house *green.htm* and the *banner* frame to start with *red.htm*.

`<NOFRAMES>`

The *Frameset* page is different from any other type of HTML page in that it has a `<HEAD>` section and a `<FRAMESET>` section but doesn't (necessarily) have a `<BODY>` section.

Look again at our compete code above. After the closing `</FRAMESET>` tag another new tag appears: `<NOFRAMES>`.

We mentioned earlier on that someone viewing your pages with an earlier version of a browser may not be able to see any frames at all. `<NOFRAMES>` allows you to insert a message or page which only they will see. By default, some editors insert something as user-friendly as:

```
"This page uses frames, but your browser doesn't support them"
```

whereas others will invite the user to download a more modern browser in order to view the page as the author intended. Nowadays, however, there are relatively few people who browse the Internet with such old browsers, so many people ignore the `<NOFRAMES>` tag.

Frame borders

If you quickly refer back to Figure 9.3, you'll see that although there are no instructions given for the width of the borders between each frame, they all default to showing quite a sizeable one. Well, the good news is that you can turn borders on or off, and you can even change their colour.

We can use two attributes to the <FRAME> tag:

- **BORDERCOLOR**
- **FRAMEBORDER**

as well as use BORDER="0" to turn borders off altogether (Figure 9.4).

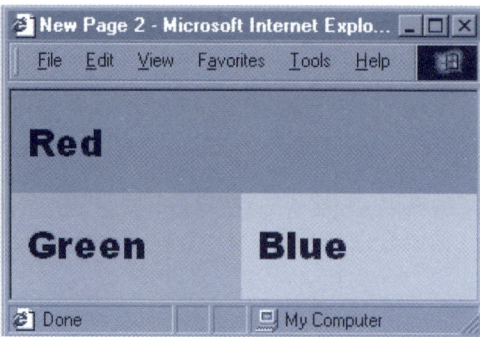

Figure 9.4 Borders between frames have been switched off.

For instance, if we wanted to have a dark red border around the middle frame in a frameset we could insert:

```
<FRAMESET ROWS="*,*,*">
<FRAME SRC="red.htm">
<FRAME SRC="blue.htm" FRAMEBORDER="1" BORDERCOLOR="dd3333">
<FRAME SRC="green.htm">
</FRAMESET>
```

You'll notice that we have made `FRAMEBORDER="1"` in order to turn the frame's border on, whilst if we had used `"0"`, the frame border would have been switched off.

Here are some more attributes for `<FRAME>`:

MARGINHEIGHT	To adjust the margin appearing above or below a frame set the number of pixels required.
MARGINWIDTH	Individually adjust the width of the left and right margins, again in pixels.
NORESIZE	To lock borders and prevent them being dragged around by your visitors.
SCROLLING="NO"	Disable the use of scrollbars within the particular frame.
SCROLLING="YES"	Scrollbars are included within the frame, whether they are needed or not.
SCROLLING="AUTO"	Scrollbars are provided only if they are needed to display the entire frame.

Note that if you set the scrolling properties to 'no', and the document contains more information than can be displayed in the available space, your viewers will not be able to scroll the additional information into view. Use this attribute with care!

Forms   10

Why forms?
What's in a form?
Buttons
Text input
Radio buttons
Check boxes
Resetting values
Selections
Form methods
CGI script

Why forms?

Up to this point we've concentrated on ways of getting information to your Web visitors. But sooner or later you will probably want to know what your visitors think, or you will want to get them to order something or even provide information to them based on characteristics that are specific to them.

This is where forms come in. A form takes information and sends it to a program running on the server – be this a CGI script, a Java program, or some other language. We'll take a very brief look at CGI later in this chapter, but many people find scripting processing programs beyond their abilities. All is not lost, however, since there are many 'free' programs out in the big wide world which can do almost anything you need doing.

What's in a form?

You won't be surprised to see that all form elements are contained in <FORM>...</FORM> tags. To change the appearance and layout of a form you will need to insert all the normal HTML layout tags; but there are additional elements, which are pertinent to forms only. If you look in your favourite Web editor you should see a selection of form elements that you can add (Figure 10.1).

10: Forms

Figure 10.1 A selection of form elements that you can add to your Web page.

Buttons

You use buttons to tell your browser to carry out tasks or to send the information contained in other fields to the processing program on the server. The label on the button is set by the *value* attribute as can be seen here:

```
<input type="button" value="click me!">
```

There's nothing to stop you having more than one button in your forms – but in this case you will have to give each one a name so that the form knows which one is being pressed (Figure 10.2):

```
<input type="button" name="button1" value="click me!">
<input type="button" name="button2" value="or click me!">
```

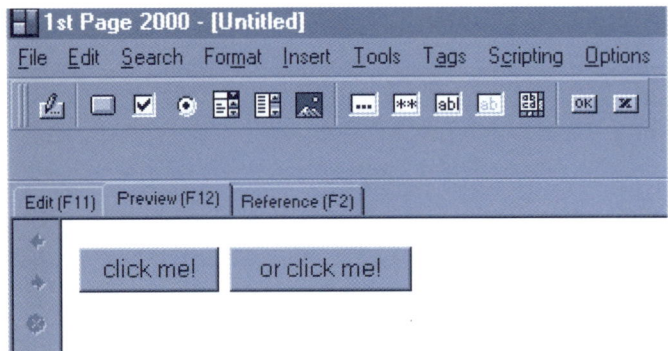

Figure 10.2 Creating two simple buttons with 1st Page 2000.

Most forms have a **Submit** button, which is used as the main way of sending information to the server.

```
<input type="submit" value="Submit Query">
```

Text input

To allow your users to type text into a single-line field you use the **TYPE="text"** attribute in the `<INPUT>` tag. You will also need to insert a NAME attribute, which will be passed to the script-processing program with the text inputted by the user:

```
<input type="text" name="newtext">
```

You can have the form display whatever field sizes you want, and can also limit the field to a maximum number of characters.

```
<input type="text" name="newtext" size="20" maxlength="20">
```

In addition to regular text fields, you can create password fields, which are identical to ordinary text fields except that whatever is typed in is displayed on screen by a line of asterisks (Figure 10.3).

```
<p> Insert your surname: <input type="text" name="surname" size="15" maxlength="20">
<p> Enter your password: <input type="password" name="pw" size="10" maxlength="10">
<p><input type="submit" value="Submit Query">
```

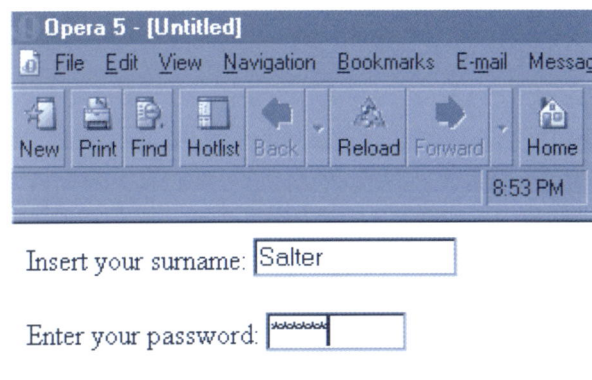

Figure 10.3 Text fields in a form.

If you want your users to be able to enter text as many lines of text, rather than just as a text-input field, you can use the `<TEXTAREA>` tag, which includes three attributes:

name The name sent to the CGI script when the form is submitted.
rows The height of the text area in rows of text.
cols The width of the text area in columns.

`<TEXTAREA>` needs a closing tag – `</TEXTAREA>` – and you can enter default text before the closing tag if you need to. You can also add default options for the text wrapping to be switched off (**WRAP=OFF**), text wrapping to be on, but the text to be sent to the server as one line (**WRAP=SOFT**) or for text wrapping to be on and sent to the server as wrapped text (**WRAP=HARD**).

```
<textarea name="your text" rows="6" cols="30" wrap=soft
>Enter some text</textarea>
```

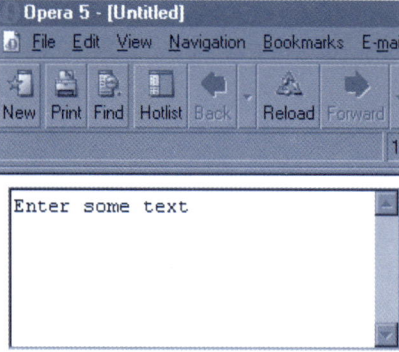

Figure 10.4 You can add some default text into the 'Textarea' tags.

Radio buttons

Radio buttons are used to display a list of choices. When one button is selected, all the others in the same group become deselected. They have **RADIO** as their type attribute and you determine each group of buttons by using a unique **NAME** attribute for the group.

So, to set up two different groups of radio choices you have to give two unique **NAME** attributes:

```
<input name="number" type="radio" value="1">1<br>
<input name="number" type="radio" value="2">2<br>
<input name="number" type="radio" value="3">3<br>
<p>
<input name="letter" type="radio" value="A">A<br>
<input name="letter" type="radio" value="B">B<br>
<input name="letter" type="radio" value="C">C<br>
```

which will appear as in Figure 10.5:

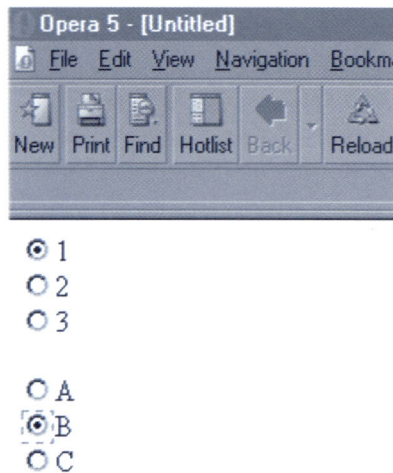

Figure 10.5 Two groups of radio buttons.

Check boxes

Unlike radio buttons, check boxes allow you to make multiple choices. Their TYPE attribute is **checkbox** and only checked boxes have their value and name pairs submitted. Unchecked boxes are ignored.

If you want to check a box by default, add the **checked** attribute:

```
<input type="checkbox" name="1" value="1" checked>1<br>
<input type="checkbox" name="2" value="2">2<br>
```

```
<input type="checkbox" name="3" value="3" checked>3<br>
<input type="checkbox" name="4" value="4">4<br>
<input type="checkbox" name="5" value="5">5<br>
```

and they should appear as shown in Figure 10.6:

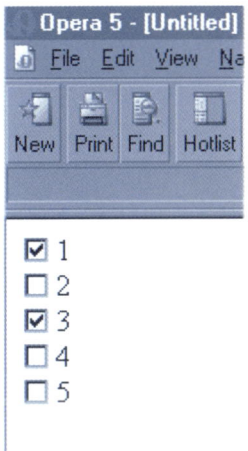

Figure 10.6 Check boxes offer multiple choices from a list.

Resetting values

We've seen that you can use the Checked attribute to set defaults for Radio buttons and check boxes. Sometimes your users might click the wrong choices on your form and wish to reset them back to the default.

You can help them by creating a **Reset** button (Figure 10.7). This has a **RESET** type and, like the **Submit** button, you can add whatever value you like.

```
<input type="reset" value="Reset back to Defaults">
```

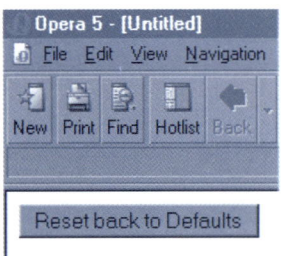

Figure 10.7 Adding a reset button.

Selections

There's another method you can use to offer your visitors multiple choices without having to spell out each option with a corresponding radio button or check box.

Drop-down menus are created using the <SELECT> and <OPTION> tags. In the same way we were able to use **Checked** to default a value of a check box or radio button, we can use **Selected** to create a default option in our drop-down menu (Figure 10.8).

10: Forms

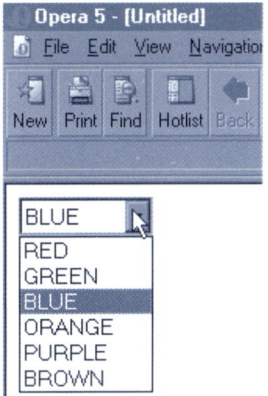

Figure 10.8 Adding 'selected' to a drop-down list.

```
<select name="COLOUR">
    <option>RED
    <option>GREEN
    <option selected>BLUE
    <option>ORANGE
    <option>PURPLE
    <option>BROWN
</select>
```

Form methods

In all this talk of forms, we haven't yet covered the two most important attributes, since what point is there in a form if you can't get the users' input to the server in the first place?

METHOD determines how your form data is sent to the server. It can take two forms:

- **Get**
- **Post.**

We'll be looking at these shortly.

The **ACTION** attribute calls the program script that processes your form's output. For instance, if you were using a CGI script it might take the form:

```
<FORM   METHOD=POST   ACTION=http://www.myISP.com/cgi-bin/
script.pl>
```

where the processing program is *script.pl*, in the *cgi-bin* directory on a server www.myISP.com.

CGI script

CGI stands for Common Gateway Interface and CGI scripts allow your visitors to interact with your Web pages. What happens when your form's **Submit** button is pressed is that the information is sent to the CGI script following the route given in the **Action** attribute. The script is run and carries out any instructions on the received data. Often this will result in outputting new data back to the browser window.

Before you can use CGI scripts in your Web pages you have to ensure that the ISP who is hosting your site can cope with such scripts. You cannot write and test CGI scripts on your local computer; you have to go through a Web server to do so.

Many ISPs insist you keep your CGI scripts in a directory called *cgi-bin* and the majority use the *Perl* programming language. It would be impossible in a book of this size to teach you how to program in Perl. However, as we have already said, there are many free programs that you can download off the Internet to help you get started, and some Web editors contain a selection of CGI scripts for you to incorporate into your Web pages (Figure 10.9).

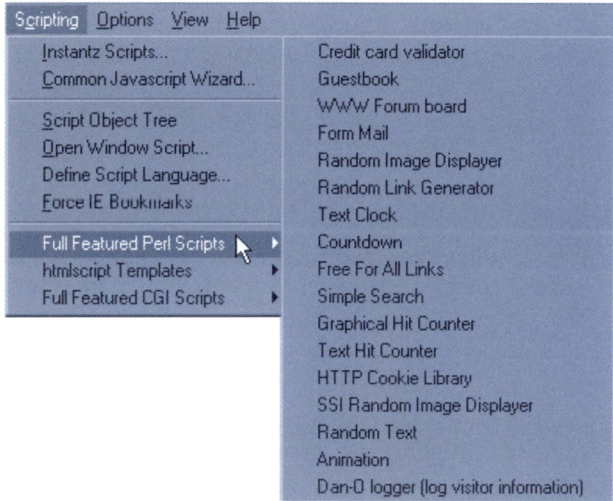

Figure 10.9 Many Web editors such as 1st Page offer pre-written CGI scripts.

You could check out a huge selection of free CGI scripts on the Web at:

- *www.free-cgi.com/*
- *http://worldwidemart.com/scripts/*
- *http://cgi.resourceindex.com/*
- *www.freecode.com/*
- *www.getcruising.com/crypt/*
- *www.dreamcatchersweb.com/scripts/*
- *www.freescripts.com/*

We mentioned a short while back that there are two types of METHOD attribute used for getting your data to the server. With **GET**, you append all the form's data at the end of the ACTION URL after a question mark:

```
http://myISP/cgi-bin/script.pl?haircolour=red&name=naomi
```

and the script takes the arguments attached after the '?'.

Obviously, if you had many arguments to pass to the CGI script, it would become somewhat ungainly to pass all the data across in a URL; so instead we use the **POST** attribute whereby all the data are sent as a separate text stream.

You may well be asking yourself if there are really no alternatives to using CGI scripts. Well, depending on what you are trying to achieve, you could use a **Mailto** form where you add your email address to the Action part of the form.

```
<FORM METHOD=POST ACTION="mailto:genius@topspin-group.com">
…</FORM>
```

When a visitor submits the form, all the arguments will be sent to you via email. However, there are a couple of downsides to this method.

1. All the data will arrive in your email inbox in encoded form. That may not matter too much, and it's usually pretty easy to import all that text into a word processor, such as MS Word, and use a search and replace routine to get rid of all the extraneous characters and thereby make it easier to read.
2. When your visitors submit the form, they won't get any confirmation that the form has actually been sent. This might cause some of them to resubmit the form. To get round this you could include a warning that they won't get any feedback, or you could use some JavaScript to warn them that something has happened.

JavaScript? Turn to the next chapter and we'll explain all!

JavaScript and DHTML

11

JavaScript structure
Sourcing JavaScript programs
Dynamic HTML
Dynamic styles
Dynamic content
Positioning and animation

HTML

*JavaScript should not be confused with Java, which is another programming language a little like C++. Java programs can run on any computer platform, but first they have to be compiled into a special form called a **bytecode**, which creates cross-platform executable files. JavaScript, on the other hand, is not a general purpose programming language, but a scripting language which extends the capabilities of the browser.*

Although this book is primarily about the workings of HTML, there are – as we have seen with CGI and style sheets, by way of example – various other elements that can be added to pure HTML code to make your pages more dynamic and to give you – the Web designer – more power to your page layouts.

One of the most commonly used add-ins nowadays found across the entire World Wide Web is the use of **JavaScript**, which is a programming language that gives a vast amount of extra functionality to a Web page.

JavaScripts are embedded in the HTML code and run within the browser environment, and in this respect JavaScript is not like CGI, which relies on the presence of a server to be able to work at all. It's a little like Visual Basic in that – in theory, at least – you can create quite complex pieces of scripting with no programming knowledge at all. Having said that, we don't have the space to teach you all there is to know about JavaScript in this book, but we will try to point you in the right direction for finding a large selection of scripts already written and just waiting for you to download from the Internet.

JavaScript structure

Before you can run a JavaScript program within a Web page, you have to declare the program to the browser, and this is done by defining the script inside `<SCRIPT>`...`</SCRIPT>` tags. These tags are normally placed in the `<HEAD>` section of the Web page, although this is not a hard and fast rule. The reason is that the program declaration is not displayed within the body of the Web page itself.

A JavaScript declaration is also written with what looks like comment tags wrapped around it, and this is because those browsers that don't understand JavaScript might otherwise try to display your code as text within the page.

So, given all the above, a Web page that contains JavaScript might have a `<HEAD>` section which takes on the following form:

```
<HEAD>
<TITLE>your title</TITLE>
<SCRIPT LANGUAGE="JavaScript">
<!--JavaScript code goes here
//this is a comment
-->
</SCRIPT>
</HEAD>
```

What happens if you want to make a comment within your JavaScript if comment tags are already used for wrapping your JavaScript code? Simply start each line within your script with two oblique slashes – // – and everything on the rest of that line will be ignored.

Sourcing JavaScript programs

Even if you don't want to get your fingers dirty with JavaScript code, it's a good idea to familiarise yourself with some of the masses of free JavaScript programs that are available on the Web. One of the best sources is www.javascript.com which not only contains scripts for just about everything you might possibly want to do, but also contains full instructions for you to copy and paste the code into your Web pages.

Here are some other sites that are well worth checking out:

- www.a1javascripts.com/
- www.cgiscript.net/site_javascripts.htm
- www.free-javascripts.com/

If you have more than one page using the same JavaScript code, you can link to that code held in a separate file by using a source attribute, thereby

>>

HTML

(Continued)

obviating the necessity of defining the script in each and every page. If the JavaScript is contained in a file called script.js then your source would look something like:

```
<SCRIPT LANGUAGE=
"JavaScript"SRC
="http://www.your
server.com/script
.js">
```

- www.iboost.com/build/programming/js/scripts/
- www.javascriptcity.com/scripts/
- www.javascript-page.com/
- www.java-scripts.net/

Remember, too, that most half-decent Web editors contain a good selection of the most commonly used JavaScripts (Figure 11.1), with the most popular one being button rollovers that change the appearance of a button when your mouse either passes over it and/or clicks on it.

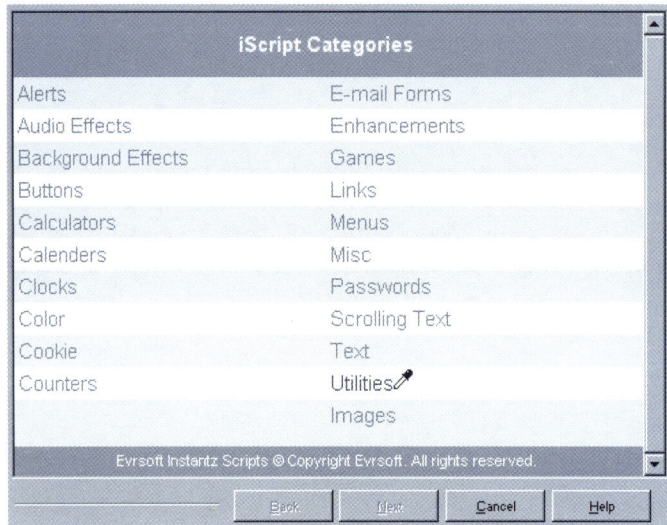

Figure 11.1 Some of the instant JavaScript categories that come free with 1st Page 2000.

Dynamic HTML

Dynamic HTML (DHTML) is an all-in-one word for Web pages that use HTML, cascading style sheets (CSS), and rely on JavaScript to make the Web pages interactive. DHTML is only found in 'later' browsers (typically version 4 and above) and relies on the browser for the display and manipulation of the Web.

The beauty of DHTML is that it creates low-bandwidth effects that can be used to create animations, games, applications, provide new ways of navigating through Websites, and create out-of-this world page layouts that are impossible with pure HTML.

Although the underlying technologies of DHTML (i.e. HTML, CSS and JavaScript) are standardised, the manner in which Netscape and Microsoft have implemented them differ dramatically. For this reason, writing DHTML pages that work in both browsers (referred to as cross-browser DHTML) can be a bit hit and miss and you will certainly need to test any code you prepare in all the main browsers.

Here is a list of just a few of the things you can achieve with DHTML:

- Hide text and images in your document and keep this content hidden until a given time elapses or the user interacts with the page.
- Animate text and images in your document, independently moving each element from any starting point to any ending point, following a path that you choose or that you allow the user to choose.
- Create a ticker that automatically refreshes its content with the latest news, share prices or other data.
- Create a form and then instantly read, process and respond to the data the user enters in the form.

DHTML achieves these effects by modifying the current document and automatically reformatting and redisplaying the document to show changes. It does not need to reload the document or load a new document, or require a distant server to generate new content. Instead, it uses the power of the user's computer to calculate and carry out changes. This means a user does not have to wait for text and data to complete time-consuming round trips to and from a server before seeing results. Furthermore, DHTML does not require additional support from applications or embedded controls to make changes. Typically, DHTML documents are self-contained, using (CSS) styles and a little script to process user input and directly manipulate the HTML tags, attributes, styles and text in the document.

Dynamic styles

Dynamic styles are a key feature of DHTML. By using styles and style sheets, you can quickly change the appearance and formatting of elements in a document without adding or removing elements. This helps keep your documents small and the scripts that manipulate the document fast.

Inline styles are CSS style assignments that have been applied to an element using the style attribute. You can examine and set these styles by retrieving the style object for an individual element. For example, if you want to highlight the text in a heading when the user moves the mouse pointer over it, you can use the heading's inline style to enlarge the font and change its colour, as shown in the following example.

```
<HTML>
<HEAD><TITLE>DHTML Mouseover Example</TITLE>
```

```
<SCRIPT LANGUAGE="JavaScript">
function doChanges() {
 window.event.srcElement.style.color = "green";
 window.event.srcElement.style.fontSize = "30px";
}
</SCRIPT>
<BODY>
<H3  ID=heading  onmouseover="doChanges()"  STYLE="color: black;font-size:18">Hover over me!</H3>
<P>Try hovering your mouse over the heading.
</BODY>
</HTML>
```

In this example, the process (known as an event handler) responds when the on-screen cursor moves over an HTML tag (which contains an **onmouseover** statement) and receives control when the user first moves the mouse pointer into the heading. The handler uses the **srcElement** property of the event object to determine which element is the source of the event – in this case, the H3 element. It then uses the **color** and **fontSize** properties of the style object for the element to change the colour and text size. Setting these properties changes the CSS colour and font-size attributes given in the style attribute for the heading, and the browser immediately updates the onscreen text to display these new attribute values (Figure 11.2).

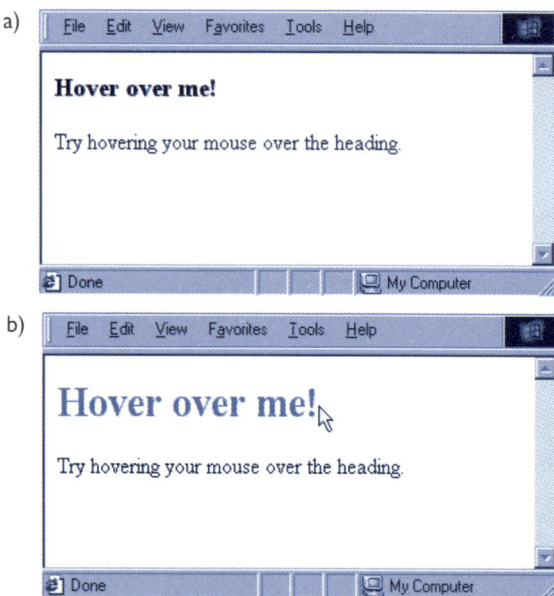

Figure 11.2 Using DHTML to change the appearance of text when you hover with your mouse.

By using styles, you can create a simple document, such as the following, in which all items in a bulleted list are hidden until the user clicks the mouse (Figure 11.3).

11: JavaScript and DHTML

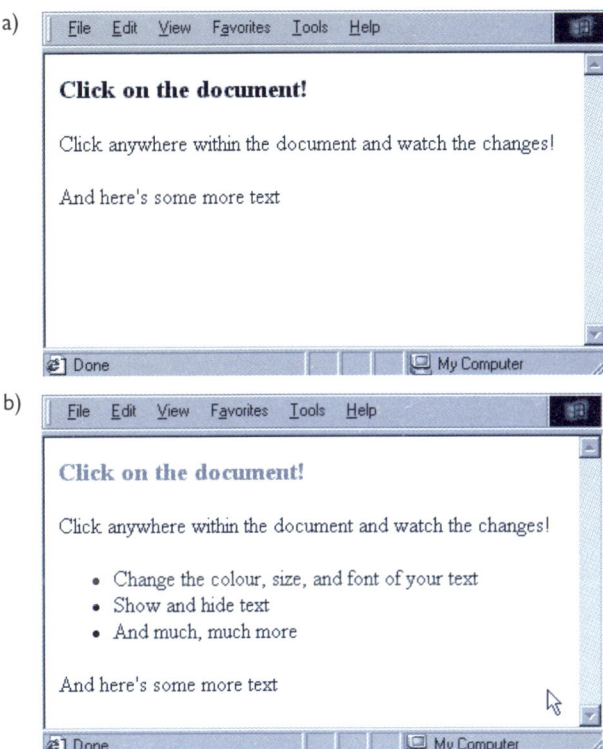

Figure 11.3 Using DHTML to change the page on a mouse click.

```
<HTML>
<HEAD><TITLE>DHTML Styles Example</TITLE>
<SCRIPT LANGUAGE="JavaScript">
function showText() {
    MyHeading.style.color = "red";
    MyList.style.display = "";
}
</SCRIPT>
<BODY onclick="showText()">
<H3 ID=MyHeading>Click on the document!</H3>
<P>Click anywhere within the document and watch the changes!
<UL ID=MyList STYLE="display:none">
<LI>Change the colour, size, and font of your text
<LI>Show and hide text
<LI>And much, much more
</UL>
<P>And here's some more text
</BODY>
</HTML>
```

In this example, the CSS display attribute is set to none, causing the UL list to be hidden from view. When the user clicks the mouse, the event handler clears the value of this attribute, making the browser display the list onscreen. Notice how any content that comes after the list shifts to accommodate the new text rendering.

Dynamic content

With DHTML, you can change the content of a document after it is loaded. The DHTML Document Object Model (DOM) provides access to all elements in the document. Consider the following simple example. You can replace and change elements as well as change colours and text by using a few lines of script (Figure 11.4).

```
<HTML>
<HEAD><TITLE>Yet Another DHTML Example</TITLE>
<SCRIPT LANGUAGE="JavaScript">
function changeText() {
    MyHeading.outerHTML = "<H1 ID=MyHeading>Pure Magic!
    </H1>";
    MyHeading.style.color = "green";
    MyText.innerText = "Brought to you with DHTML.";
    MyText.align = "center";
    document.body.insertAdjacentHTML("BeforeEnd", "<P ALIGN =\"center\">Try it now!</P>");
}
</SCRIPT>
```

```
<BODY onclick="changeText()">
<H3 ID=MyHeading>Yet Another DHTML Example</H3>
<P ID=MyText>Click anywhere on this page.</P>
</BODY>
</HTML>
```

a)

Yet Another DHTML Example

Click anywhere on this page.

b)

Pure Magic!

Brought to you with DHTML.

Try it now!

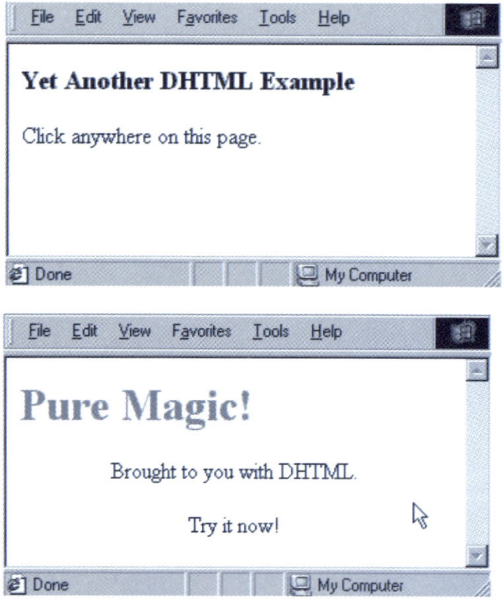

Figure 11.4 Replacing text with DHTML.

When the user clicks on the page, the script replaces the H3 element with an H1 element, centres the paragraph, and inserts a new paragraph at the end of the document. Using script in this way, you can add, delete and replace any elements and text in the document.

Positioning and animation

Positioning is the ability to place an HTML element at a specific point in a document by assigning an x- and y-coordinate and a z-plane to that element. This means you can place elements – images, controls and text – exactly where you want them and achieve special, overlapping effects by defining in what order elements at the same point should be stacked on top of one another.

Positioning is an extension of CSS. This means that you set the position of an element by setting the appropriate CSS attributes for that element. The following example shows how to set the absolute position of an image.

```
<HTML>
<HEAD><TITLE>Positioning</TITLE>
<BODY>
<H3>Positioning with DHTML</H3>
<P>With positioning, you can place images exactly where you
want them, even behind text and other images.
<IMG STYLE="position:absolute;top:0; left:0; z-index:-1"
SRC="image.gif">
</BODY>
</HTML>
```

In this example, the image is placed at the document's top left corner. Setting the z-index attribute to –1 causes the image to be placed behind the text on the page (Figure 11.5).

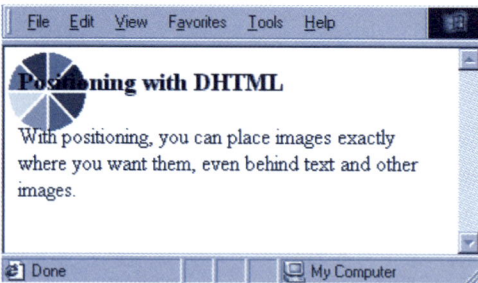

Figure 11.5 Absolute positioning with DHTML.

But now try changing the values of *top* to 30 and *left* to 100. Now when you load the page into your browser you should find it looking like Figure 11.6.

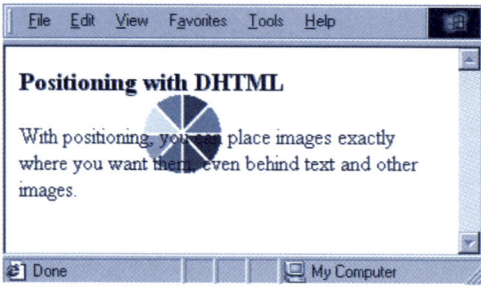

Figure 11.6 Determine the absolute position in relation to the top left-hand corner of the page.

We could go on for many pages giving typical examples of how clever DHTML is, but to try it out for yourself, use an HTML editor such as Dreamweaver or FrontPage (Figure 11.7) and investigate the effects that they offer, before then heading off to the Web and accessing some of these sites:

- www.dynamicdrive.com/
- www.dhtmlshock.com/
- www.24fun.com/
- www.bratta.com/dhtml/scripts.asp
- www.astentech.com/scripts/DHTML.html

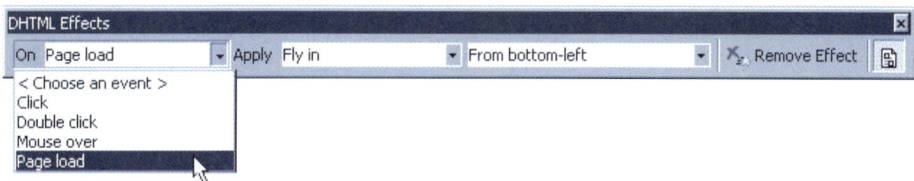

Figure 11.7 Adding DHTML effects using MS FrontPage.

Meta tags 12

What are meta tags?

General tags

Format

DC tags

Other tags

What are meta tags?

Right, now you've created a killer Website and you've FTP'd it up on to the Net. But how will anyone know where to find you unless you tell the search engines that your site exists?

The newer search engines such as Google (www.google.com) use robots known as *spiders* that continuously trawl across the Web looking for new sites and keywords that it can use to catalogue your site. When you've connected to a search engine you will almost certainly have seen that the results are formulaic – in other words there is usually a site title, followed by a short description of the site (Figure 12.1). Sometimes, instead of a title and description you will see displayed what appears to be the main text of the page.

What is going on? Why are some entries different from others?

The answer lies in the use of what are generally known as **meta tags**. And the entries in the search engine returns that look like straight page text are exactly that: text straight off the Web page being catalogued.

To help the search engines in their relentless trawl of Websites, Web authors usually use these meta tags to flag up their sites to any passing spider. By doing this, they can ensure that keywords describing the site are picked up, and that the title and short description of their site in the search engine's displayed pages will accurately reflect what is on the site, rather than relying on the search engine's spider to do the job for them.

Meta tags are not visible to the site visitors – well, certainly not in the browser window anyway, although if you go into the source code for the HTML file you will normally see the meta tags listed in the `<HEAD>` section.

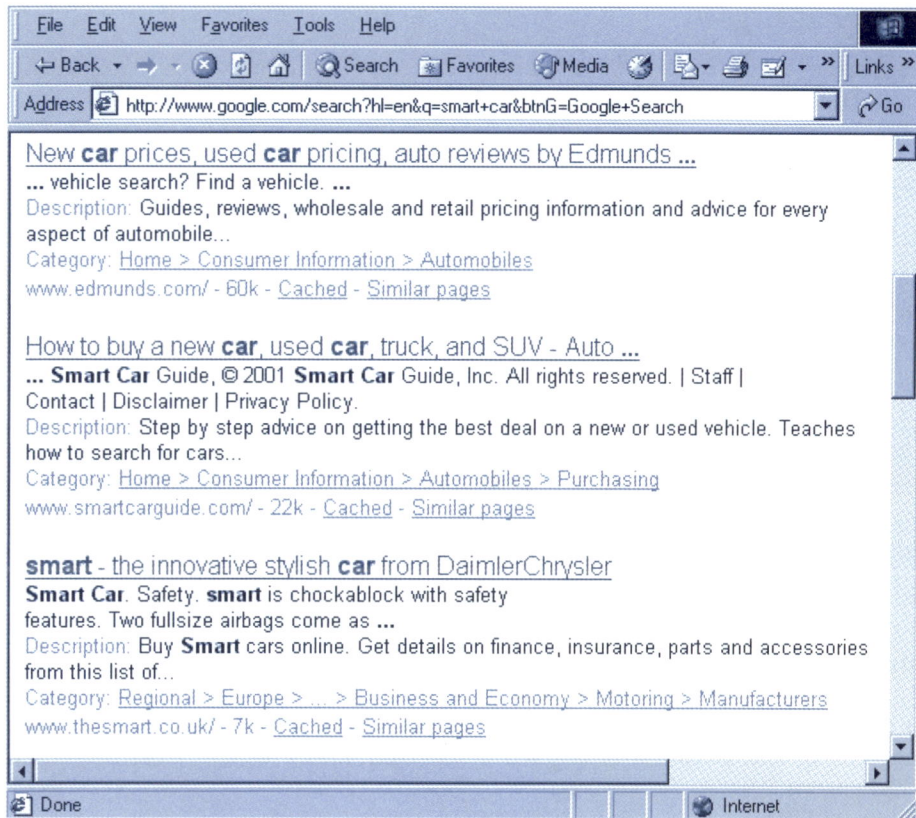

Figure 12.1 Search engines such as Google use meta tags to capture content information.

General tags

The three most important meta tags which no self-respecting Web author should do without are:

- **Title**
- **Description**
- **Keywords.**

Their roles are quite obvious really. The title content is what will appear in the search engine results and will act like a headline in a newspaper, flagging up a viewer's interest for your site as opposed to anyone else's site.

The description should ideally be a one-liner, giving a very brief description of what the site is all about. In theory you can have as many as 200 words in a description, but do you really think the prospective visitor is going to wade through so much text in order to see if your site is for him? Besides, many search engines chop the text if it is longer than a certain length – typically running up to two lines.

Keywords are used to flag up to the search engines the keywords on your site to correspond with words the user enters into the search engine. Your well-crafted site might mention the newts in the pond at the bottom of your garden, but if you were trying to sell garden plants, you would be better off putting in some of the plant names as your keywords to make the search more relevant and faster. Keywords should be separated by commas, with the most important words listed first.

Format

Meta tags are constructed of three sections:

- The **Attribute** specifies whether it contains descriptive information about the page (name) or HTTP header information (http-equiv). The latter can supply special instructions to a Web browser, such as an expiration date or a display-refresh value.
- **Value** then specifies the type of information you're supplying in this tag. In theory you can specify practically any value you like.
- **Content** is the actual information.

Let's look at a typical set of basic meta tags:

```
<HTML>
<HEAD>
<meta http-equiv="Content-Type" content="text/html; charset
=iso-8859-1">
<META NAME="keywords" CONTENT="newts, fish, ducks, water-
lilies">
<META NAME="description" CONTENT="a site about the joys of
owning a garden pond">
<META NAME="author" CONTENT="naomi langford-wood">
<META NAME="copyright" CONTENT="2002">
<META NAME="revisit-after" CONTENT="1 month">
```

Most Web editors have the capability of inserting meta tags (Figure 12.2), so if you're at all worried about the correct usage, they will do it all for you.

Here, you see the two types of meta tags. The majority have a simple **name** attribute, followed by the **value** (e.g. *keywords*, *description*, etc.) followed by **Content** which describes the tag in question. The first meta tag, however, gives information not about the content of the site, but about its construction – hence it has a **http-equiv** type of tag.

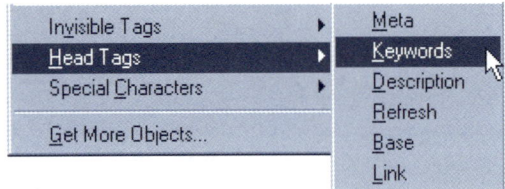

Figure 12.2 Dreamweaver includes the most commonly used meta tags in its Insert menu.

Confused? Well, let's see a list of some of the other types of meta tag available…

Author	This represents the name of the person who authored the page.
Email	The contact person's email address.
Copyright	The copyright year and the name of holder.
Revisit	This sets the frequency of a spider's return.
Refresh	This field must contain a URL that refers the page to another link in a specified number of seconds.
Expires	The date when the content expires.
Distribution	Global – Used for major entry points.
	Local – Used for local entry points.

Robot	Web spiders can be restricted using the following Robot meta tags:
All – Robots may traverse and index the page;
No Index – Robots may traverse but not index the page;
No Follow – Robots may index the page but not follow it;
None – Robots may neither index nor traverse the page.
Content rating	General
14 Years
Mature
Restricted.

Remember that none of these meta tags are visible on your Web page. They are only there for information, which can be picked up by either the server or the browser.

DC tags

There is another set of meta tags known as **Dublin Core** which are used to supplement existing methods for searching and indexing Web-based meta data. Dublin Core meta tags are mostly used by universities and government institutions that catalogue large libraries of information.

If you want further information on these types of tag, visit www.dublincore.org.

DC.Title	This is the name of the resource.
DC.Description	An account of the resource's content.
DC.Creator	The primary creator of the content.

D.C.Subject	The topic of the resource's content.
DC.Publisher	The one who makes the resource available.
DC.Contributors	Contributor to the resource's content.
DC.Date	Date of the resource's creation.
DC.Type	Nature of the resource's content.
DC.Format	Media type of the resource.
DC.Identifier	URL of the resource.
DC.Source	Source from which resource derived.
DC.Language	Language of the resource's content.
DC.Relation	Reference to a related resource.
DC.Coverage	Geographic scope of the resource's content.
DC.Rights	Information about rights held in the resource.

Other tags

If you haven't totally switched off by now, there are even more meta tags you can come up with. As we saw above, it's quite common to show which character set (*charset*) your site has been constructed with, especially if it is not in a mainstream European language.

The most common character set is ISO-8859-1, and here is a rough list of the languages contained in the ISO 8859 series.

ISO-8859-1 Afrikaans, Basque, Catalan, Danish, Dutch, English, Faeroese, Finnish, French, Galician, German, Icelandic, Irish, Italian, Norwegian, Portuguese, Spanish and Swedish.

ISO-8859-2   Latin-written Slavic and Central European languages.
ISO-8859-3   Esperanto, Galician, Maltese and Turkish.
ISO-8859-4   Scandinavia/Baltic.
ISO-8859-5   Cyrillic.
ISO-8859-6   Arabic.
ISO-8859-7   Modern Greek.
ISO-8859-8   Hebrew.

If you're at all worried by meta tags it is probably best to stick to the golden three:

- Title
- Description
- Keywords

and not worry about any of the others.

If you do want to experiment with them, however, you can't do better than use a freeware utility called Metty which you can download from www.clickfire.com (Figure 12.3).

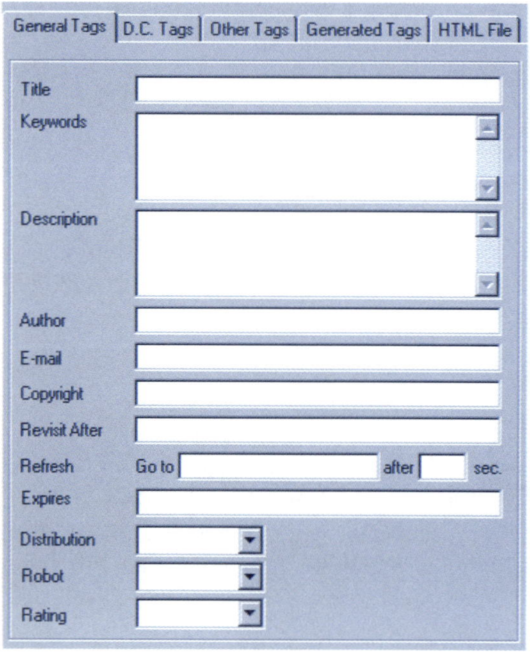

HTML

Figure 12.3 'Metty' offers you more tags than you could ever possibly dream about.

Appendix

HTML colour equivalents

Appendix: HTML colour equivalents

Colours in HTML come in two flavours: *named colours* and *hex numbers representing colours*. Any colour you want to use is made up of varying proportions of red, green and blue. Each of these three colours can have a value of anything from 0 to 255, which gives a total of 16.7 million possible shades available.

The corresponding hex numbers are given here for each named colour, and you can enter either into your HTML documents – the tag `<FONT COLOR=FF0000>` means just the same as `<FONT COLOR=RED>`.

Name	Hex	Name	Hex
AliceBlue	F0F8FF	Burlywood	DEB887
AntiqueWhite	FAEBD7	CadetBlue	5F9EA0
Aqua	00FFFF	Chartreuse	7FFF00
Aquamarine	7FFFD4	Chocolate	D2691E
Azure	F0FFFF	Coral	FF7F50
Beige	F5F5DC	CornflowerBlue	6495ED
Bisque	FFE4C4	Cornsilk	FFF8DC
Black	000000	Crimson	DC143C
BlanchedAlmond	FFEBCD	Cyan	00FFFF
Blue	0000FF	DarkBlue	00008B
BlueViolet	8A2BE2	DarkCyan	008B8B
Brown	A52A2A	DarkGoldenrod	B8860B

Name	Hex	Name	Hex
DarkGray	A9A9A9	ForestGreen	228B22
DarkGreen	006400	Fuchsia	FF00FF
DarkKhaki	BDB76B	Gainsboro	DCDCDC
DarkMagenta	8B008B	GhostWhite	F8F8FF
DarkOliveGreen	556B2F	Gold	FFD700
DarkOrange	FF8C00	Goldenrod	DAA520
DarkOrchid	9932CC	Gray	808080
DarkRed	8B0000	Green	008000
DarkSalmon	E9967A	GreenYellow	ADFF2F
DarkSeaGreen	8FBC8F	Honeydew	F0FFF0
DarkSlateBlue	483D8B	HotPink	FF69B4
DarkSlateGray	2F4F4F	IndianRed	CD5C5C
DarkTurquoise	00CED1	Indigo	4B0082
DarkViolet	9400D3	Ivory	FFFFF0
DeepPink	FF1493	Khaki	F0E68C
DeepSkyBlue	00BFBF	Lavender	E6E6FA
DimGray	696969	LavenderBlush	FFF0F5
DodgerBlue	1E90FF	LawnGreen	7CFC00
Firebrick	B22222	LemonChiffon	FFFACD
FloralWhite	FFFAF0	LightBlue	ADD8E6

Name	Hex	Name	Hex
LightCoral	F08080	MediumBlue	0000CD
LightCyan	E0FFFF	MediumOrchid	BA55D3
LightGoldenrodYellow	FAFAD2	MediumPurple	9370DB
		MediumSeaGreen	3CB371
LightGreen	90EE90	MediumSlateBlue	7B68EE
LightGray	D3D3D3	MediumSpringGreen	00FA9A
LightPink	FFB6C1		
LightSalmon	FFA07A	MediumTurquoise	48D1CC
LightSeaGreen	20B2AA	MediumVioletRed	C71585
LightSkyBlue	87CEFA	MidnightBlue	191970
LightSlateGray	778899	MintCream	F5FFFA
LightSteelBlue	B0C4DE	MistyRose	FFE4E1
LightYellow	FFFFE0	Moccasin	FFE4B5
Lime	00FF00	NavajoWhite	FFDEAD
LimeGreen	32CD32	Navy	000080
Linen	FAF0E6	OldLace	FDF5E6
Magenta	FF00FF	Olive	808000
Maroon	800000	OliveDrab	6B8E23
MediumAquamarine	66CDAA	Orange	FFA500
		OrangeRed	FF4500

Name	Hex	Name	Hex
Orchid	DA70D6	Sienna	A0522D
PaleGoldenrod	EEE8AA	Silver	C0C0C0
PaleGreen	98FB98	SkyBlue	87CEEB
PaleTurquoise	AFEEEE	SlateBlue	6A5ACD
PaleVioletRed	DB7093	SlateGray	708090
PapayaWhip	FFEFD5	Snow	FFFAFA
PeachPuff	FFDAB9	SpringGreen	00FF7F
Peru	CD853F	SteelBlue	4682B4
Pink	FFC0CB	Tan	D2B48C
Plum	DDA0DD	Teal	008080
PowderBlue	B0E0E6	Thistle	D8BFD8
Purple	800080	Tomato	FF6347
Red	FF0000	Turquoise	40E0D0
RosyBrown	BC8F8F	Violet	EE82EE
RoyalBlue	4169E1	Wheat	F5DEB3
SaddleBrown	8B4513	White	FFFFFF
Salmon	FA8072	WhiteSmoke	F5F5F5
SandyBrown	F4A460	Yellow	FFFF00
SeaGreen	2E8B57	YellowGreen	9ACD32
Seashell	FFF5EE		

Index

\# 29, 79
& 29
  99
! 13
!-- 14
/p 23

A
A 68, 72–3, 75, 141
ABOVE 117
absolute path names 70–1
ACTION 162
ADDRESS 27
AIFF (Audio Interchange File Format) 59
aligning text 30–1
   with images 39–43
   with style sheets 133–4
   in tables 109
ALL 117
ALT 49–50, 78
alternative text 49–50

ampersand (&) 29
anchors 68, 72–3, 75
animation 169, 177–9
Apple QuickTime 63
applets 64–6
AREA 77, 78
arrow characters 29
Audio Interchange File Format (AIFF) 59
author contact details 27
AVI (Audio Video Interleave) files 63

B
B 25
background colours/images 50–1, 106–9, 125, 129–31
background music 58–9, 61–2
banner frames 138, 141, 144
BASE 144
BELOW 117
BGCOLOR 51, 106–7
BGSOUND 61–2

BIG 25
BLOCKQUOTE 27
BODY 12, 13
BODY BACKGROUND 51
bold text 25
bookmarks 72
BORDERCOLOR 109
borders
   frame borders 148–50
   for image hotspot 76
   and style sheets 131–3
   for tables 105, 117
BOX 117
BR 24
browsers 2–7
   colour displays 4
   fonts 4, 21
   interpretation of tags 6–7
   Microsoft Explorer 2–3, 4
   Netscape Navigator 2–3, 4 5–6
   Opera 2–3
   upgrades 3
   viewing HTML code 10

Index

bulleted lists 87–90
button rollovers 168
buttons 153–4
bytecode 166

C

CAPTION 101–2
cascading style sheets 120, 127, 169
CELLPADDING 103
CELLSPACING 104–5
CENTER 31
centred text 30–1
CGI (Common Gateway Interface)
    scripts 162–4
cgi-bin 163
character set 188–9
check boxes 158–9
citations 27
CITE 27
class files 65–6
CLEAR 45
CODE 27
code samples 27
CoffeeCup 11, 14
colours 4, 33, 192–5
    background colours/images 50–1,
        106–9, 125, 129–31
    BORDERCOLOR 109
    in tables 106–9

COLS 117
COLSPAN 111, 112
comment tags 166–7
Common Gateway Interface (CGI)
    scripts 162–4
Composer 7
computer code samples 27
contents frame 138, 141
Courier 25, 28
CSS *see* cascading style sheets

D

data tags 97–8
DC (Dublin Core) meta tags 187–8
DD 91
definitions 27
DFN 27
DHTML *see* dynamic HTML
directories 70
DIV 31
DL 91
DOM (Dynamic Object Model) 175
Dreamweaver 7, 10, 11–12, 14
drive letters 70
drop-down menus 160
DT 91
Dublin Core (DC) meta tags 187–8
dynamic content 175–7
dynamic HTML 169–79

Dynamic Object Model (DOM) 175
dynamic styles 170–5

E

editors *see* text editors; Web editors
EM 27
email addresses 74
embedded style sheets 121, 125–6
emphasised text 27, 28
excape codes 74
event handlers 171
EvrSoft 1st Page 2000 7, 10–11, 13
external style sheets 121, 122–3

F

file formats 36, 59–60
filenames
    absolute path names 70–1
    case sensitivity 69
    drive letters 70
    for images 38
    relative path names 69–70, 71
1st Page 2000 7, 10–11, 13
Flash movies 63–4
folders 70
fonts 4, 21, 132–3
    non-proportional 25
    sizes 31–2
    see also colours

Index

footers 113–16
foreign characters 29
forms 152–64
   ACTION 162
   buttons 153–4
   CGI scripts 162–4
   check boxes 158–9
   and DHTML 169
   GET 162, 164
   Mailto forms 164
   METHOD 162, 164
   password fields 155
   POST 162, 164
   radio buttons 157–8
   reset buttons 159–60
   selection lists 160–1
   sending 162
   Submit buttons 154, 162
   text input 154–6
FRAME attributes in tables 116–18
frames 138–50
   absolute values 146
   banner frames 138, 141, 144
   BASE 144
   borders 148–50
   contents frame 138, 141
   main frame 138, 141
   NOFRAMES 146–7
   NORESIZE 149
   scrollbars 149–50
   TARGET 140–4
framesets 140–1, 144–6, 147
FrontPage Express 7, 10, 14

G

Get 162, 164
GIF (Graphical Image Format) 36
glossary lists 91–2
Google 182, 183
graphics *see* images
GROUPS 117, 118

H

hash sign (#) 29, 79
HEAD 12, 13, 126
headers and footers 113–16
heading cells in tables 101–2
heading levels 20–2
hiding text 169, 172–5
highlighting text 170–1
horizontal rules 51–6
hotspots 75–6, 78
HR 52–6
HREF (Hypertext Reference) 68–9
HSIDES 117
HSPACE 46
HTML 12, 13
hyperlinks *see* links

I

I 25
Imagemaps 76–9
images 36–56
   aligning text/headers with 39–43
   alternative text 49–50
   backgrounds 50–1, 106–9, 125, 129–31
   Border 76
   file formats 36
   filenames 38
   height and width 48
   hiding 169
   horizontal rules 51–6
   as links 75–6
   low resolution 48–9
   optimising 36–7
   positioning 39–41, 177–9
   previews 48–9
   scaling 48
   software 36–7
   source filenames 38
   spacing 46–8
   text wrapping 43–6
IMG 38–41, 76

Index

indexing pages 21
inline style sheets 121, 134–6, 170
INPUT 154
Internet Explorer 2–3, 4
ISO 8859 character set 188–9
italicised text 25

J
Java applets 64–6
Java programs 166
JavaScript 164, 166–8
   comment tags 166–7
   linking code 167–8
JPEG (Joint Photographic Experts Group) 36

K
KBD 27
keywords 184

L
left justified text 30–1
LHS 117
LI 82, 83, 85–6
line-height 133
line returns 23
line wrapping *see* wrapping text
lines 51–6

LINK 122
links 68–79
   absolute pathnames 70–1
   anchors 72–3
   bookmarks 72
   HREF (Hypertext Reference) 68–9
   Imagemaps 76–9
   images as 75–6
   mailto: command 74–5, 164
   NAME 71
   relative pathnames 69–70, 71
   special characters 73–4
   to specific locations 72–3
   to Web pages 71
lists 82–93
   bulleted 87–90
   glossary 91–2
   nesting 92–3
   numbered 82–7
low resolution images 48–9
LOWSCR 48

M
Macromedia
   Dreamweaver 7, 10, 11–12, 14
   Flash technology 63–4
   Shockwave technology 63–4
Mailto 74–5, 164

MAP 77
margins 127–9
mathematical symbols 29
menus 160
meta tags 14, 182–90
   DC (Dublin Core) meta tags 187–8
   descriptions 184
   format 185–7
   keywords 184
   title content 184
METHOD 162, 164
Metty 189, 190
Microsoft
   Explorer 2–3, 4
   Front Page Express 7, 10, 14
   Word 16
MIDI (Musical Instrument Digital Interface) files 59
MP3 (Motion Picture Experts Group Audio Layer-3)files 60
MPG (Motion Picture Experts Group) files 63
multimedia 58–66
   Flash movies 63–4
   Java applets 64–6
   Shockwave movies 63–4
   sound 58–62
   video 63

N

NAME 71
named entities 29
nesting lists 92–3
Netscape
   Composer 7
   Navigator 2–3, 4, 5–6
newlines 24
NOFRAMES 146–7
non-proportional fonts 25
NONE 118
NORESIZE 149
Notepad 8
NOWRAP 106
numbered entities 29
numbered lists 82–7

O

OL 82, 84
onmouseover 171
Opera 2–3
OPTION 160
ordered lists 82–7
overlapping effects 177

P

P 23–4
padding 103–5, 127–9
paragraphs 22–4
password fields 155
path names *see* filenames
Perl programming language 163
PNG (Portable Network Graphics) 36
positioning images 39–41, 177–9
POST 162, 164
PRE 28
preformatted text 28
previewing images 48–9

Q

QuickTime 63
quotations 27

R

radio buttons 157–8
Real Audio 60
REL 122
relative pathnames 69–70, 71
reset buttons 159–60
RGB values 33
RHS 117
right justified text 30–1
Robot meta tags 187
ROWS 118
ROWSPAN 111, 112
RULE attributes in tables 116–18

S

S 25
SAMP 28
sample text 28
scaling images 48
SCRIPT 166
scrollbars 149–50
search engines 21, 182
SELECT 160
selection lists 160–1
SHAPE 77
Shockwave movies 63–4
SMALL 25
sound 58–62
   background music 58–9, 61–2
   download times 58, 61
   file formats 59–60
   linking to audio files 58
   looping 61
   stereo balancing 61
   volume 59, 62
spaces 28, 46, 133
           99
   in URLs 74
SPAN 136
special characters 28–30, 73–4
spiders 182
stereo balancing 61

strikethrough text 25
STRONG 28
STYLE 126
Style Master 121
style sheets 120–36
   alternative 122
   backgrounds 129–31
   borders 131–3
   cascading style sheets 120, 127, 169
   declaration 120
   default 122
   dynamic styles 170–5
   embedded 121, 125–6
   external 121, 122–3
   fonts 132–3
   inline 121, 134–6, 170
   margins 127–9
   padding 127–9
   persistent 122, 123
   selector 120
   text alignment 133–4
SUB 25
Submit buttons 154, 162
subscripts 25
SUP 25
superscripts 25

T

tables 96–118
   alignment attributes 109
   borders 105
   colours 106–9
   footers 113–16
   FRAME attributes 116–18
   headers 113–16
   heading cells 101–2
   padding 103–5
   RULE attributes 116–18
   sizing 103–5
   spanning across rows and columns 109–13
   text layout 105–6, 109
tags
   case sensitivity 20, 69
   comment tags 166–7
   data tags 97–8
   for heading levels 20
   interpretation by browsers 6–7
   see also meta tags
TARGET 140–4
TBODY 113–16
TD 98, 113
text 20–33
   alternative text 49–50
   character set 188–9

headings 20–2
hiding 169, 172–5
highlighting 170–1
layout in tables 105–6, 109
logical styles 26–8
new lines 24
paragraphs 22–4
physical styles 25–6
preformatted 28
special characters 28–30
see also fonts
text alignment 30–1
   with images 39–1
   with style sheets 133–4
   in tables 109
text editors 8
text input 154–6
text wrapping 22–3, 43–6, 156
   NOWRAP 106
TEXTAREA 156
TFOOT 113–16
TH 98, 101–2, 113
THEAD 113–16
tickers 169
TITLE 15
TopStyle 121
TR 97
TT 25

U

U 25
UL 88
underlined text 25
unordered lists 87–90
URLs (Uniform Resource Locators) 71, 73–4
USEMAP 79

V

VALIGN 109
VALUE 86
VAR 28
variables 28
video 63
VOID 117
volume control 59, 62
VSIDES 117
VSPACE 46

W

watermark 51
WAV (Waveform Extension) files 59
Web editors 7–12
    HTML view 10
white spaces *see* spaces
Word 16
word processors 15–17
wrapping text 22–3, 43–6, 156
    NOWRAP 106

For where to go, who to read and what to know in the world of IT.

If you're looking for books on IT then visit: **www.it-minds.com**, the place where you can find books from the IT industry's leading IT publishers.

[Choice of publishers]

IT-Minds is home to some of the world's leading computer book publishers such as Sams, Que, Addison-Wesley, Prentice Hall, Adobe Press, Peachpit Press, Cisco Press and Macromedia Press.

[Choice of ways to learn]

We publish for those who are completely new to a computer through to the most cutting-edge technologies for the IT professional and our products offer a variety of ways to learn. IT-Minds offers you tutorials, handy pocket guides, comprehensive references, exam guides, CD based training materials and Executive Briefings.

[Choice of subjects]

We also cover the A-Z of computer subjects: From ASP, Bluetooth, C++, Database, E-Mail, Flash, Graphics, HTML ... to Windows XP, XML, Yahoo and Zope.

Infinite choices for the IT Minded

As an IT mind you also have access to:

- News from the IT industry
- Free weekly newsletters
- Articles written by our featured authors
- Competitions to win prizes
- Testing and assessment products
- Online IT training products

[Custom Solutions]

If you found this book useful, then so might your colleagues or customers. If you would like to explore corporate purchases or custom editions personalised with your brand or message, then just get in touch at **www.it-minds.com/corporate.asp**

Visit our website at: [**www.it-minds.com**]